TAKING YOUR PLACE
at the TABLE

Praise for

TAKING YOUR PLACE
at the TABLE

Joseph Bensmihen offers real insight, guidance, and inspiration for moving you, or your business, from the outside to the inside.

—**Michael A. Boylan**, author of *The Power to Get In* and
Accelerants

Having built up his own health-care business with uncommon courage and determination, Joseph proves that when God deals you a lousy deck, you can turn it into all aces. His perseverance, irrepressible spirit and will to win, as well as his unshakable belief that nothing's going to get in his way, have inspired everyone who knows and works with Joseph.

—**Warren Struhl**, founder of Paper Direct, Popcorn Indiana, and Polaroid Fotobar, and author of *Starting Them Up*

JB Bensmihen shares his life with the reader in a straightforward, engaging way. His book is a personal reflection, but also a guide for being thoughtful, thinking and persevering, while focusing on achievement.

—**Richard M. Joel**, President, Yeshiva University

TAKING
YOUR PLACE
at the
TABLE

The Art of Refusing to Be an Outsider

Joseph JB Bensmihen

NEW YORK

LONDON • NASHVILLE • MELBOURNE • VANCOUVER

TAKING YOUR PLACE *at the* TABLE
The Art of Refusing to Be an Outsider

Published in New York, New York by Morgan James Publishing. Morgan James is a trademark of Morgan James, LLC. www.MorganJamesPublishing.com

The Morgan James Speakers Group can bring authors to your live event. For more information or to book an event, visit The Morgan James Speakers Group at www.TheMorganJamesSpeakersGroup.com.

ISBN 978-1-68350-452-8 paperback
ISBN 978-1-68350-453-5 eBook
Library of Congress Control Number: 2017902024

Cover Design by:
Rachel Lopez
www.r2cdesign.com

Interior Design by:
Bonnie Bushman
The Whole Caboodle Graphic Design

In an effort to support local communities, and raise awareness and funds, Morgan James Publishing donates a percentage of all book sales for the life of each book to Habitat for Humanity Peninsula and Greater Williamsburg.

Get involved today! Visit
www.MorganJamesBuilds.com

To my mother
Alegrina "Abouela" Bensmihen
for making something so extra ordinary look simple.
You made motherhood look effortless, yet you knew the
challenges ahead before anyone else.

and to
Karina Bensmihen
my best friend and cheerleader

and to
Maurice, Kayla, Rena, and Henry Bensmihen
You are the first people I want to speak to in the morning
and the last people I want to hear from before I go to sleep.

I love you,
JB

Table of Contents

Introduction

Don't Wait for Others
to Offer You a Chair

This book is about belonging.

We all need to belong. And the truth is that each of us—you, me, everyone—already *does* belong. But not everyone knows it or believes it.

There will always be people—including people in authority—who will tell you that you don't belong. Some will tell you that you don't *deserve* to belong. They couldn't be more wrong.

This book is about taking your place at the table, no matter what other people say.

You may have heard of me because of my work. I've advised members of Congress from both sides of the aisle, as well as many other elected officials. I've spoken before the US House Committee on Education and the Workforce. I've met with three US presidents, a Canadian prime minister, and lots of other key leaders.

Many people, though, have heard of me for an entirely different reason: I've been instrumental in helping people—especially political leaders—understand how to treat human beings with disabilities.

This began when I was six years old, when I met with prime minister Pierre Trudeau. I was in the news five years later, when I became the first disabled Canadian student to be mainstreamed in a public school. The press coverage turned international when I gave the valedictorian speech at my high school graduation. At age 22 I was back in the news again, when the Americans with Disabilities Act went into effect and I published a widely discussed opinion piece for the *Montreal Gazette*, urging Canada to follow America's lead. Because of these efforts, I've sometimes been described as a political activist, but I've never really thought of myself that way. I've just tried to be a voice of reason.

I was born with cerebral palsy. I walk with two canes, but I'm fast and in good shape, so I have no trouble keeping up with other people. When I'm standing at a podium or seated, my disability is invisible.

But when I was growing up in Montreal, I wasn't allowed to go to a regular school with my friends from my neighborhood or synagogue. Instead, I had to go to a special school—a place for what we kids called cripples and retards. This made no sense to me. When I asked my father why this was so, he said, "It's the law."

So I asked my father to drive me to Ottawa. I told him I wanted to talk to Prime Minister Pierre Trudeau about the law. To his great credit, he did.

I was six. I didn't know that people weren't supposed to just walk into the prime minister's office to ask questions. So—wearing leg braces and using two canes—I did, with my father behind me.

I got lucky: Trudeau was in his office, and he invited me inside. We talked most of an hour, and I explained why I wanted to go to school with my friends. And eventually the laws in both Canada and the United States were rewritten so that people like me were "mainstreamed"—sent to the same schools as other children.

I'll tell this story in more detail later in this book. My point is that, from the time I was six, I knew that I belonged, and I couldn't understand why some people thought that I didn't. I wanted my place at the table.

Although this book is partly about me, it's mostly about you. Whatever table you want to sit at, this book can help you get there. It offers advice, guidance, inspiration, and real-life stories about what works and what doesn't.

I don't know your specific situation or skill set. But I do know this: we all belong somewhere.

Each table is different. Places at some tables are earned. At others, they're inherited or received as gifts. At still others, they're purchased for hard cash. (Far more are acquired in this way than most people realize.)

Places at other tables have to be fought for and won, through debate or persuasion or an election.

Many people don't realize that to take your place at some tables, all you have to do is walk up and sit down. If you can't walk, then roll up in a wheelchair.

You probably won't need to change national or state laws to take your own place at many tables. But, like I did, you may need to challenge, or stare down, or ignore the people who say you don't belong. You might need to ask them why they think you don't deserve a place. You might need to simply motion them aside and slip your own chair in. You might also need to say, "I'm here—and I'm not leaving."

This book offers inspiration, guidance, strategies, stories, and practical advice for taking your own place at any table where you genuinely belong.

I don't mean to suggest that you're entitled to sit at any and every table that attracts you. Some tables will be out of reach because of your skill level or income or background. I'm no exception in this regard. I had to learn the hard way—by going to law school, studying as earnestly as I could, and not being able to keep up—that I wasn't cut out to be a lawyer. I also know that the Catholic Archdiocese of Miami is not going to let a somewhat-observant Jew like me help them run their organization, no matter what skills I have.

We all have limitations. I don't know what yours are. But I do know that there is often a world of difference between your actual limitations and the limitations that people think or say or believe you have. It's important to understand your real ones. It's just as important to question the ones that other people—or you—merely imagine.

Why should you listen to me instead of some other disabled man or woman who does a lot of public speaking? Here's why:

Over the years I've sat at many important tables. I'm the former president of the Private Care Association, a national association that supports consumer choice in private health care and the rights of caregivers who serve those consumers. I'm a member of the national council of the American Israel Public Affairs Committee. I direct the David Bensmihen Charitable Foundation, which provides scholarships for deserving students. For the past five years I've been a member of the Board of Overseers for the men's undergraduate college at Yeshiva University. Until 2014, I was the CEO of United Elder Care Services, which provided home care to elderly and disabled people in south Florida. After selling that business, I became the Executive Director of VIP Care Management, a full-service geriatric care management company in Lake Worth, Florida. Today I'm Vice President of Evergreen Private Care and live in St. Petersburg.

I've never stopped questioning and challenging rules that don't make sense to me. In this book, for example, you will read about some other instances where I took a very public stand on important issues. In these cases, I had to do much more than just walk into someone's office. I had to file lawsuits, educate key leaders, provide testimony, and ask just the right questions. Above all, I had to be strategic. As a result, I won the day each time.

I'm a somewhat-observant Sephardic Jew. This means that I follow many (but not all) of the customs and practices of centrist Orthodox Judaism. For two years, I was the president of one of the largest synagogues in the American southeast; for seven I was on the Board of Governors of the Orthodox Union. But I'm not beholden to Orthodox thinking. I make up my own mind about what matters and what it means to live a good Jewish life. I'm also a firm believer in letting each person—observant Jew, non-observant Jew, Christian, Muslim, or otherwise—pray however they want to pray. Taking your place at any religious table doesn't mean leaving your good judgment, or your compassion for other human beings, at the door.

I've advised—and been advised by—conservatives, liberals, and moderates. I've had dinner with each of the last three former presidents, two of them Democrats, and I've met our current president, a Republican. Later in this book, I'll say plenty of good—and not-so-good—things about both parties. Taking your place at any political table doesn't mean checking your ethics or principles with your coat. Though it does often mean opening your wallet—sometimes very wide.

Although I've said this book is mostly about you, it's also about everyone. It's for anyone who wants to succeed at work or in life. It's for anyone who has ever been (or felt) excluded. And it's for anyone who wants to belong—which is everyone.

Getting to the table is only a means to an end. Once you're there, you'll have important work to do, using your place at that table to serve other human beings. That's why the table is there in the first place. (If not, please find a different table.) This book will help you serve others more effectively.

It's also important to help and support the others at the table, as well as the people who want and deserve a place at it, but have not gotten there yet.

If this is the type of role you envision for yourself, then welcome. You've come to the right place.

Pull up a chair. If the chair has wheels, wheel it up. Let's get started.

Part 1

GETTING TO THE TABLE

1

When Other People Say You Don't Belong at the Table, Ask Them to Explain Why

When I was six years old, growing up in Montreal, I wanted to go to a regular school—the same school that my seven-year-old sister attended. Some of my friends from the neighborhood and my synagogue went there, too. The school was just down the street, a two-minute walk away.

But I wasn't allowed to go there. Instead, I was put into the Mackay Center for Crippled and Disabled Children, an hour-long bus ride away.

That's because back then, in 1976, I wore leg braces, like the young Forrest Gump. I also walked with two canes. From my feet to my thighs, I was different from most kids. Otherwise, though, I was just like them.

But I *was* very different from many of the kids at Mackay. Some couldn't control their bladders; some had very low IQs; some had debilitating illnesses.

I asked my parents, "Why do I have to go to school at Mackay? My brain works fine. My mouth and ears and eyes work fine. I don't pee in my pants. I just walk funny."

"We know, Joseph," my parents said. "We're sorry. But it's the law." This made no sense to me.

I asked my teachers the same question. "It's the law, Joseph," they told me. "And we need to follow the law."

"But what if the law is stupid?" I asked. "And what if I *want* to go to a regular school, like my sister?"

"It doesn't matter," they said. But it mattered to me.

No one seemed to care or pay attention to what I said. So, during my fourth month at Mackay, I picked up a desk and threw it out the window.

Suddenly, *everyone* started paying attention to me. I was sent to see a school psychologist. He wanted to know why I threw the desk out the window, so I told him. Finally, someone was listening.

The psychologist met with my parents. He said, "I'm afraid your son has psychological issues. He can't accept the reality of being here in this school."

My father David, of blessed memory, responded this way: "My son doesn't have any issues. He just doesn't want to be here. And I don't blame him. He told me he thinks the law doesn't make sense, and I agree with him."

The next day I asked my father, "Who made that crazy law?"

"I'm not sure," my dad said. "Probably the federal government in Ottawa."

"Is that where the prime minister lives?" I asked.

"That's right."

"Can we drive to Ottawa and talk to him?"

"Sure," my father said.

"Okay!" I said. "Let's go right now."

"Grab your coat. I'll get the car."

Now I ask you: how many other fathers would say yes to that request?

We got in the car and drove to Ottawa, which was two hours away. We parked a couple of blocks from the Langevin Block, where Prime Minister Trudeau had his office, and walked into the lobby.

What do you do when you want to get backstage at a rock concert— or go anywhere else where you might not be allowed? You act like you belong and walk like you know where you're going. If you do that— even if you're wearing leg braces and walking with two canes—nobody's going to bother you. I don't know how I intuited this at age six, but I did. I just kept walking, and my dad walked beside me. We didn't ask anyone for directions, and we didn't slow down.

There were security guards, but no one tried to stop us. No one even said anything. They probably thought, *Hey, there goes a cute kid with leg braces and canes. He and his dad are probably tourists, visiting Parliament. That's great.*

We got to the prime minister's office and walked right into the reception area. I went up to the receptionist's desk and said, "I'd like to see the prime minister, please."

There were security guards in the outer office, of course, and suddenly they were standing right next to me. One of them asked, "How did you get in here, son?"

I pointed to the door. "We walked down the hall and came in. It wasn't locked."

The receptionist smiled at me and said, "What's your name?"

"Joseph."

"Well, Joseph," she said, "the prime minister's very busy right now."

Six year olds are not known for their tact or their patience. I raised my voice. "But I want to talk with him! My dad and I just drove two whole hours to get here, and I want him to answer my questions!"

The security guards could have easily picked me up and carried me out of there. But that's not what happened. The door to Pierre Trudeau's inner office opened and he came out. "What's going on?" he asked.

"I want to talk to you about my school," I said.

A tall man hurried over and stood between Trudeau and me. I was told later that he was the prime minister's chief of staff. "I'm sorry, sir," he said. "I don't know how he got in here."

Trudeau waved him off. "Don't be sorry," he said. "This young man's got something to say. I want to talk to him. Come on in." He motioned to my father and me, and we went into his office and sat down on a sofa across from his desk.

He asked me my name, and I told him. "All right, Joseph," he said, "tell me what's on your mind."

"Look," I said, "there's some law that I think you're in charge of, and it says that I can't go to the same school as my sister. I don't understand why that is. She goes to the school right by our house, and I have to ride a bus for almost an hour to Mackay. Some of the other students there can't speak or think or learn much of anything. Some of them have to wear diapers. But I can speak and think and learn and hold in my pee, just like my sister. Please let me go to the same school she does. Or at least explain to me why I can't."

Trudeau asked, "Where do you live, Joseph?"

"In Laval." Laval is the city just north of Montreal.

He nodded. "I'll need to check on this, but I think it's probably a provincial law. Let me see what I can do."

"So you'll help me?" I asked.

"I'll look into it, Joseph. You have my word."

Later, as we drove back to Montreal, my father said, "Joseph, you did well. You were a real inspiration."

"Do you think the prime minister will help me?" I asked.

"Honestly, Joseph, I don't know," my dad said. "But it's possible."

But this meeting was of course only the beginning.

·⟐· OTHER KEY LESSONS ·⟐·

- When a rule, law, or regulation doesn't make sense, ask people why it's there. If their explanation also doesn't make sense, try to change the rule.

- When people aren't listening, find a way to get their attention. But don't throw large objects out windows, except as a last resort (and even then only if you're six years old or younger).

- When you need assistance, approach the highest-ranking person you believe can help.

- Don't let impressive-sounding titles or official-looking buildings intimidate you.

- Don't be afraid to speak up. And if you are afraid, speak up anyway, in spite of the fear.

- Be clear about exactly what you want or need.

- If your child asks for your help in making the world better—even if their plan sounds strange or crazy—think twice before saying no. If there's no risk of harm, think very seriously about saying yes.

2

When People Say There's No Room at the Table, Don't Believe Them

Pierre Trudeau turned out to be right. The decision where I would go to school wasn't up to him, but to the school board of the province of Quebec.

The school board couldn't ignore my request. For one thing, the prime minister was now involved. All he probably did was say to an aide, "Ask the Quebec school board to look into this," but of course that was enough.

In June of 1977, about a year after I tossed that desk out the schoolroom window, the Quebec school board decided that I could go to a regular school. But this decision wasn't about making things better for disabled people in general. The school board's decision was strictly about me and me alone.

The laws about mainstreaming kids with disabilities and normal brains—and about protecting disabled people in general—wouldn't be passed for another 14 years in the United States, in 1990. In Canada, it would take another 21 years—until 1998—to amend the Canadian Human Rights Act so that it gave people with disabilities some legal protections. Even today, there is still no Canadian equivalent of the Americans with Disabilities Act, on either the national or the provincial level.

In essence, the school board said, "Joseph can go to a regular school. If anyone else with a disability wants to do the same, they'll have to come to us, just like Joseph did, and we'll make our decisions on a case-by-case basis."

On the one hand, the status quo hadn't changed. But on the other, a legal precedent had been set. The door had been opened a crack, and I wedged my foot in the opening—leg brace and all—and began pulling the door open.

Although I wanted to go to the same school as my older sister, the Quebec school board sent me to a school that was further away but smaller. They felt that I'd do better at a smaller school with fewer students. I was okay with that. What mattered was that it was a regular school.

But what I didn't know was that, even at the regular school, there was something called special education. This was a separate class for kids who weren't considered smart enough to keep up in a normal classroom. In Canada at the time, many of the special ed students were hockey and basketball players—talented athletes who didn't worry about their grades.

I didn't understand why the adults in charge thought that this was where I belonged. I certainly wasn't going to be an athlete. Or did people think that, because I walked funny, I couldn't think properly?

I'm not saying these adults couldn't think properly themselves. They may have put me in special ed because I had to have lots of orthopedic surgeries, and missed a lot of school as a result. I eventually had 14 operations. This often meant breaking and resetting bones. Back then, the recovery time from one of these operations was a month. I also had to spend at least an hour a day doing physical therapy. So the adults probably thought, *We don't want to set Joseph up for failure. Let's make things a little easier for him by putting him in special ed.*

And the truth was that, at first, this didn't really bother me. For the first two years or so, I was happy to just be in a regular school.

But by the fifth grade, I'd had it with special ed. I knew I wasn't learning as much as most students. I didn't want a second-rate education. So I said to the principal of the school, Mr. Rooney, "I want to be in a regular classroom."

He said, "I'm sorry, Joseph. You can't do that."

I asked him to explain why.

He said, "It's never been done. Regular classrooms aren't set up for you."

Even at that young age, I knew that, just because something hadn't been done before, that didn't mean it couldn't be done now. In 1969, the year I was born, human beings landed on the moon. That hadn't been done before. For the past few years, a kid from Montreal who walked funny had attended a regular school instead of the Mackay Center for Crippled and Disabled Children. That hadn't been done before, either.

So I said to my father, "I want to be in a regular classroom. Will you help me get there?"

He didn't even have to think about it. "Sure," he said.

This time, though, we knew it wasn't a simple matter of applying pressure and getting permission. We had to have a plan. We had to find a way for me to keep up in a regular classroom. There were only 24 hours in a day, and we would have to find a way to fit everything in.

First we talked it over with my mother. She was fine with the idea, but she was adamant: no matter what, I was not going to give up Hebrew school or bar mitzvah lessons. I and my father were fine with this.

Then we went to my orthopedic surgeon. He said to me, "Joseph, you're one of my smartest patients. You have my blessing to do anything you want, so long as you figure out a way to include physical therapy in your daily regimen."

In Quebec, every child studies both English and French, regardless of what language their family speaks at home. My parents were both from Morocco, where most people speak French, and my whole family spoke fluent English, French, and Spanish at home. (My parents also spoke Italian and Arabic.) So we figured out that if I could get dispensation to not take French class, I could instead go to the local YMCA and swim every day. That would be my physical therapy. And then everything else would fit into my day.

My father took this proposal to Mr. Rooney, who at first rejected the idea. But my father didn't give up; for six weeks, he kept pushing and pressuring Mr. Rooney to agree. My father was never aggressive or angry, but he had a reputation for being relentless about causes he believed in—and he certainly believed in me. Eventually Mr. Rooney said yes.

But there were two catches.

Catch #1: Mr. Rooney knew that I hadn't gotten as good an education in special ed as most students in regular classrooms had. So he insisted that, instead of going into the sixth grade the following year, I would repeat fifth grade in a regular classroom. I had no problem with this, and neither did my parents.

Catch #2: I would have to prove myself. At the end of the following school year, I'd have to take a big, province-regulated math test, designed specifically for me. If I failed the test, I probably would be sent back to special ed—probably for the rest of my school years.

All of this put me in the news again. *Remember the disabled boy who met with the prime minister a few years ago and convinced the Quebec school board to move him to a regular school? Well, he's won the day again.*

At the time, I didn't understand what the fuss was about. I felt that I was a kid with a normal brain in a normal school who was finally getting put in a normal classroom. But suddenly there were television cameras in my face.

There was also a twist to some of the media stories. They asked, *Are Joseph's parents really being intellectually honest by allowing him to go into a regular classroom? He's going to fail. Is this really fair to him?* Other people pushed back and said, *Hey, the switch doesn't even happen until fall. Give the boy a chance. He can think and reason and talk just fine. Maybe he'll do well.* People started taking sides.

But I didn't. I ignored both sides of the chatter. My attitude was, *People can think and say whatever they like. But I'm going to learn in a regular classroom in the fall.*

My first day in a regular classroom was tough. I could tell that some of the teachers felt I didn't belong. One teacher in particular seemed to have it in for me. To spare her embarrassment, I'll call her Mrs. Copley. When I sat down in her class on that first day, she looked at me grimly and said, "What are you doing here?"

I said, "What do you mean? I'm in school."

"Who said you could be here?"

That made me very nervous. "I don't know," I said. "My dad."

"Your dad doesn't work here."

"Okay, then. The principal."

I thought, *Uh oh. I hope it gets better.*

And after that one difficult moment, things generally did get better. For the most part, being in a regular classroom was fine. After the first few days, most of the teachers and kids accepted me, and I was able to get good grades and keep up with the subjects we studied. Mr. Rooney, the principal, also seemed to want me to succeed.

The one big exception was Mrs. Copley, who taught us math and several other subjects. From the way she treated me, I knew she wished she could get rid of me.

As my father and I had arranged, I took all the regular subjects except French, during which I went swimming. After school, I went to Hebrew school. I stayed home when I was healing from surgery, as well as during the major Jewish holidays, like almost all my Jewish classmates. Otherwise, I went to the same classes as all the other kids.

The real test, though, would be toward the end of that school year. I mean that literally. In May, I'd have to take that all-important math exam. I wasn't worried, because I'd studied hard and hadn't had any problems in math throughout the year. My grades were fine and I understood all the key concepts I'd been taught.

Because I was the first disabled child in Canadian history to learn in a regular classroom, the media were watching me. Would I pass the test, and prove to the world that mainstreaming some disabled kids was a good idea—as well as the right thing to do? Or would I fail, and "prove" to the media that kids with any kind of disability—even one that had nothing to do with cognitive skills—simply couldn't keep up?

The day of the test arrived. Two impressive-looking men in trench coats showed up from the board of education. They put me in a separate room and made me take the test alone. To this day I don't understand why. Did they think I was going to cheat somehow? Were they worried that media people were going to barge into the testing room while I was taking the exam?

They handed me the test booklet, and I opened it and started working.

The first problem was easy. The second was tougher. And then something strange happened: many of the problems veered off into the unknown. I didn't understand some of the symbols or what I was supposed to do with them. I didn't even understand some of the questions.

In all, about half the test covered familiar material. The other half involved concepts and symbols that Mrs. Copley never once talked about in math class.

As I handed in my completed test, I knew that I was in trouble.

My score on the exam was 48 out of 100. I had failed miserably.

The news spread quickly throughout the community. Some people suggested that I had been a noble but ill-advised experiment that had failed. Others said, in essence, "This is why we have laws that protect crippled people, by keeping them apart from the rest of society."

I was sitting on my bed, crying, when my father came in. He put his hand on my shoulder and asked me one simple question: "Joseph, what happened? We had this in the bag. How could you not have been ready?"

Through my tears, I said, "I don't know, Dad. I never learned half the stuff on the exam. I mean, I knew what they were—fractions, percentages, decimal points—but Mrs. Copley never taught us how to work with them."

My father said, "If you never learned it, how do we know if any of the other students in your class did? Call one of your friends and ask him if he learned all the stuff on the test."

So I called my friend Arthur. I said, "Arthur, I didn't understand how to work with half of what was on my math exam. I can't figure out what happened."

I heard Arthur take a deep breath. "Okay," he said. "I'm not supposed to tell you this. But while you were away for the Jewish holidays, Mrs. Copley taught us a lot of this stuff. And when you would go to the Y to swim, and you thought we were studying French, she was actually teaching us math. She switched things around so you wouldn't have a chance to learn them."

I thanked my friend, hung up the phone, and told my dad what Arthur had just explained to me.

My father's face filled with fury and determination. "Joseph," he said, in a voice that permitted no questioning or objections, "You are not going back to school for the rest of this year. You're going to stay home and study for that test. You're going to take it again, and this time you're going to pass. I'm going to make *sure* this happens. Is that clear?"

"Okay," I said.

The next day, my father called the school principal, at home. I don't know exactly what he told the principal, but he got Mr. Rooney to agree to give me a new math test at the very end of the school year. Meanwhile, I was going to stay home and study for it.

My father owned six drapery stores in and around Montreal. Normally he spent 50 to 70 hours a week at these stores. But he told his employees, "I need you to run things without me for the next six weeks." For those weeks, instead of going to work, he stayed home with me and spent all day coaching me for the test.

My father guessed—correctly, as it turned out—that the test would be based on my math book. So we went through the book page by page, from beginning to end, over and over. Eventually I memorized the entire book in the same way that children in some synagogues might have to memorize their Torah portions for their *bar mitzvot*.

On the very last day of the school year, just as my dad had arranged with Mr. Rooney, I went back to school. My friends were all glad to see me, which made me feel good.

Although lots of media had covered me when I took the math test the first time, none showed up for the retest. That was fine by me. This time, too, there were no board of education people in trench coats. Mrs. Copley was the one who gave me the exam. But she put me alone in the same room, just like before.

This time I knew everything on the exam. I finished it in 25 minutes. But because I was allowed an hour and a half, and I didn't want to freak out Mrs. Copley, I sat quietly for another 40 minutes or so. Then I got up and went to her classroom, where she was alone, working on final grades.

She nodded at me. "All right, Joseph, you can go. I'll look this over later."

Somehow I knew that the right thing to do was act like my father. "No," I said. "Now is good."

She glared at me, but she opened the booklet and began going through it.

As she turned the pages, her lips and jaw tightened and her expression grew more and more upset. Finally she stood up and slammed her pencil on her desk. "You got a 98," she said angrily. Then she left the room and started running down the hall at top speed toward Mr. Rooney's office.

I went out into the hall. As she neared Mr. Rooney's office, she started screaming, *"Where's the other test? WHERE'S THE OTHER TEST?"* Then she turned the corner and was gone.

Not knowing what else to do, I went back into the classroom and sat down.

About 20 minutes later, Mr. Rooney came into the classroom—without Mrs. Copley. He smiled at me. "Joseph," he said, "come with me to my office, please."

A few minutes later I was seated across from him at his desk. I had no idea what he was going to say or do, but I was so bewildered that I hardly cared. "Listen, Joseph," he said. "I was watching you when you handed in that first test, the one where you got a 48. I could tell from the expression on your face that something was wrong, very wrong. Later, when you said that you never learned the material, I could see that you were telling the truth."

He paused and sighed. "Joseph, what do you see when you look at me?"

Now I was even more confused. "I see the principal, Mr. Rooney. The man in charge."

He nodded. "That's not what a lot of people see. All they see is my black skin—and it scares them. They don't think of me as a school principal. They think of me only as a black man, and they have all kinds of false assumptions about what that means.

"In the same way, some people—even some teachers—look at you, and all they see is your disability. It's sad, but that's how it is." He leaned forward. "Because of my skin, I've experienced discrimination, just like you have. I've watched how certain teachers have treated you, and I understand how you must feel because of it.

"Now, I don't know exactly what went on with that first test, but I knew that something wasn't right. That's why, when your father called and said, 'I want you to let Joseph take the math exam again,' I said okay. And that's also why, that night, I took your first test home and I burned it."

He stood up and held out his hand. "Congratulations, Joseph. It's not often that boys become men at your age. You're mature beyond your years. It's my pleasure to announce your graduation to sixth grade."

When word got out about my eventual success, people stopped me on the street and said, "Way to go," or "You're a great guy," or "You did good things; thank you." Mothers who saw me in a store would tell me about their children who had disabilities.

Now, finally, the issue was no longer just about Joseph. The dominoes had begun to fall. The provincial government started to relax its stance on educating disabled students. It realized that its laws were antiquated and needed to be updated.

These changes took two forms. The first was to create a place for disabled but mentally capable people in regular schools and regular classrooms. Now, if you couldn't walk or move your arms or see, but your brain was fine and you wanted to be in a regular school, you could go to one. The second was to rethink the special education classrooms within those schools. Up until then, they had been a place to park the athletes and the students with low mental abilities. The school board re-envisioned special ed as a place where people with disabilities could be accommodated, and where people could set and reach specific goals.

So if you were like me—if you walked funny or couldn't walk at all, but otherwise you were fine—you could go into a regular classroom. If you were blind, or couldn't move your arms, or couldn't speak, then you could still go to a regular school, but into special ed, where you'd be accommodated—but where you were also expected to learn and achieve.

Thankfully, special education is no longer a dumping ground for people whom our educational system decided to partly ignore. Instead, it has become like pre-boarding an airplane.

When a commercial flight is ready to accept passengers, airline employees first board people with disabilities, and anyone else who needs special assistance. These passengers are on the same plane as everyone else, and they have to follow the same in-flight regulations. They're simply given a chance to get on the plane at their own pace, and (if necessary) with assistance.

Similarly, in today's special ed, students receive the same education as everyone else, and are expected to live up to the same standards. But they are given the opportunity to work at their own pace—and assisted by the reasonable accommodations they might need.

~~ OTHER KEY LESSONS ~~

- When people tell you, "You've pushed enough boundaries," pay no attention. Wherever there's a boundary that doesn't serve people, it needs to be pushed aside or dismantled.
- When you're fed up with something, say so to the people in charge. Otherwise they may never realize—or care—that you're dissatisfied.
- "It hasn't been done" is not a valid reason to keep on not doing something. *Nothing* was ever done until someone did it.
- Sometimes you have to make a plan to make things work.
- When you have to, be very assertive and very persistent— but never aggressive or angry.
- When people take sides and start chattering at each other, ignore the chatter and stay focused on your goals.
- Every transformation begins with a single domino falling.

3

Getting a Place at One Table Will Help You Get a Place at Another

Now it was official: I could stay in a regular classroom in a regular public school.

But by then—the end of my second year of fifth grade—I was ready to change schools again.

I'd been in a school for the disabled; a special ed classroom in a regular public school; and a normal classroom in a regular public school. Each new option had been better than the one before. But for me, even in a regular classroom in a normal public school, something was missing.

From the time I was a child until quite recently, I was *frum*. That's a Yiddish word meaning *observant* or *devout*. This doesn't mean acting rigid or showy or holier-than-thou. It just means wanting to study Torah and live a good—and observant Jewish—life.

So, right after I passed the math test, I told my parents, "I want to go to Hebrew Academy in the fall."

After all the time my father had spent to keep me in a regular public school classroom, you'd think this might have ticked him off. But it didn't at all. "Great," both my parents said immediately. "We're behind you."

Hebrew Academy was where many observant Jews in Montreal went to school. It offered an excellent education in both traditional academics and Jewish studies. But from the time it was founded through fall of 1981, it had never educated a single student with a disability.

This was partly understandable. For one thing, the Jewish community in Montreal had done almost nothing to advocate for kids with disabilities. For another, the Hebrew Academy building had four stories and no elevator. But I could handle the stairs, as long as I went slowly. As I often told people, "I might walk funny, but I can walk."

I also knew that I'd always been able to go to school where I wanted to in the past. I'd broken through two barriers; why not three?

As it turned out, number three was easy. Maybe it was because the laws and practices in the public schools had already started to change. Maybe the directors of the school were half expecting my application, since by now I was pretty well known (and in some people's eyes, something of a hero). Either way, I was quickly admitted. No one put up any fuss or asked any questions (other than "You can do the stairs, right?").

At Hebrew Academy I had my first true mentor, a teacher named Glenna Chinks. She was 23 or 24, and it was her first year as a teacher. She cared about me deeply, took me under her wing, and gave me lots of help and attention. Her personal mission was to make sure I succeeded, and to help make me as strong a student as possible. She was a great teacher, but she was also like an older sister to me.

At first I wondered why she took such an avid interest in me. Eventually she told me: she was engaged to the gym instructor from my previous school. Back when they were first dating, he would sometimes tell her about the kid with leg braces and two canes. He explained that some of the teachers felt this disabled kid didn't belong there, and that a few of them tried to set up the kid to fail. She never dreamed that this same kid would eventually show up in her own classroom. But there I was. And from the beginning, she said to herself, *Some of my predecessors tried to crush Joseph. I'm not going to let them win. I'm going to rehabilitate him and bring him back to life.*

For the entire next year, Glenna Chinks carried me on her wings and helped me be a very successful student. She was kind and concerted, and she was my consistent advocate.

At Hebrew Academy graduations, there were three valedictorians; one gave a speech in Hebrew, one in English, and the third in French. All three valedictorians were chosen by their peers. My classmates voted me to be the French valedictorian. I was also given the school's *midot tovot* award for exemplary kindness and conduct.

In addition, in that year Hebrew Academy created a new award for community service, which it gave me for my activist work on behalf of Jews from Ethiopia, Soviet Union, and elsewhere. (More on this later.)

The Canadian Broadcasting Corporation sent a camera crew to my graduation to cover my speech. Although almost all of that speech was in French, I deliberately said this one line in English so it would be understood by the largest possible audience: *I think I've proven that society has the handicap, while the individual only has a disability.* As I'd hoped, that line was picked up, played, and replayed by a wide range of media outlets and feeds.

In my speech, I also thanked my entire graduating class—not just for supporting me, but for genuinely wanting every student to succeed.

When I received my diploma, everyone clapped, cheered, and gave me a standing ovation.

When I tell this story to live audiences, here is how I end it:

One of the greatest basketball players of all time, Michael Jordan, says that when he was in college and a scout came to watch him play, he took a shot from the half-court line. It went in. "If it weren't for that shot," Jordan tells people, "I might not have made it into the NBA."

What's the difference between Michael Jordan and people with disabilities? We don't succeed when we *make* the shot; we succeed when we *take* the shot.

But if we're serious about inviting people with disabilities to the table, then we need to do more than just encourage them to take the shot. We also need to give them the necessary support, training, and guidance to help them *make* the shot as often as possible.

And when we provide that assistance, they often make the shot— over and over, throughout their lifetimes. They also become independent and productive members of society.

❦ OTHER KEY LESSONS ❦

- Once you succeed at something, use what you've learned to succeed again and again.
- If you take the time to mentor someone, your effort and support can transform their life.
- When the media offer you a few minutes of attention, use that attention to spread your most important message.
- People have disabilities, not handicaps. But sometimes *society* is handicapped by an inability to see people for who they are.
- Thank supportive people for their support.
- Encourage and appreciate other people's success.

- Making the shot is wonderful. But there is value in simply taking the shot.
- Provide others with support, training, and guidance so they *can* make the shot.

4 Understand How a Seat at the Table Is Acquired. Some Seats Are Earned; Some Are Inherited; Some Are Awarded Or Given Away; Some Are Purchased; and Some Need to Be Fought For and Won.

Not all seats at all tables are acquired in the way people assume they are.

Let's start with board membership. Positions on many important nonprofit boards and councils are appointed, but also partly earned *and* partly paid for. (Seats on many other nonprofit boards are filled through elections, either by members or other board members.)

For example, because of my accomplishments and abilities, I was appointed to the national council of the American Israel Public Affairs Committee (AIPAC) and the board of Yeshiva University's men's undergraduate college. But with each appointment comes the expectation of a substantial financial contribution to the organization every year.

Some folks see this as an example of institutional greed, but I don't. I view it as a simple requirement that people put their money where their beliefs are. When an organization asks for and expects substantial ongoing donations from its board members, it's partly testing their commitment to the organization.

People serve on a nonprofit board for two primary reasons: 1) they genuinely believe in, and want to help advance, the organization's mission, and 2) they want to strengthen their own reputation and resume. If someone is more interested in what a board appointment can do for them than in how they can serve the organization, they shouldn't be on the board at all. Requiring a hefty financial commitment helps to weed out many of the reputation-builders.

I'm a strong proponent of Yeshiva University, AIPAC, and all the other organizations on whose boards I've served. But if I hadn't been offered places at their governing tables, I'd still have made substantial contributions (though, in some cases, not quite as substantial) to them.

That said, there's often a difference between getting on a board and staying on it.

Imagine that you've been on a board or council for some years, and have provided the organization with plenty of valuable guidance, ideas, leadership, or simple hard work. Let's also imagine that you've recently had some financial troubles. You say to the board chair, "I'm sorry, but this year I can only give a quarter of what I've contributed in the past. When I'm in a better position financially, I'll be happy to resume making larger contributions." There's a good chance that the chair's response will be, "Your service is deeply important to us. We don't want to lose you over money. Please stay on the board and make whatever financial contribution you can."

As I've learned, getting elected to public office sometimes involves backroom deals. The kind of deal I'm referring to is both legal and ethical, though not always transparent to voters. Such deals don't involve campaigning or voting, but simply getting (or staying) on the ballot.

Here's one example. In 2014, I announced my candidacy for a seat in the Florida Senate. I challenged Ellyn Bogdanoff in the Republican primary for the right to face off against Democratic state senator Maria Sachs in November. But Republican leaders didn't want the expense and trouble of a primary. They urged me to withdraw from the race, and they offered me this deal: if I bowed out gracefully, and let Bogdanoff be their anointed one, the party would anoint me for a different office in a later election. In essence, they told me, "Be an outsider now and we'll make you an insider later."

Let me be clear: I wasn't forced out, or given an ultimatum or a financial bribe to withdraw. All of those would clearly have been illegal. Nor could the party absolutely promise me that I would run unopposed in a future primary—only that it would make the same efforts on my behalf that it was making on Bogdanoff's now. But the party's offer amounted to a very powerful incentive to back out—and a deal that seemed very much worth taking. I took it and withdrew.

The Republican Party kept its word. In 2016, it backed me in my run for a seat in the Florida House of Representatives in District 68, which includes part of St. Petersburg and its suburbs. And guess who else backed me? Ellyn Bodganoff.

In the United States, getting elected to national office is full of contradictions. Getting on the ballot is often surprisingly easy. In some states, to run for a U.S. Senate or House seat, you simply pay a filing fee (as little as $50), or collect the requisite number of signatures (as few as 100), or both. This is why you often see people with no relevant credentials, skills, or chance of winning on your election ballot.

Furthermore, in locales that lean heavily blue or red, if you are a credible candidate aligned with the less-powerful party, it is often possible to skip the primary and become the automatic general-election candidate.

But to actually get elected to Congress—or, increasingly, a state legislature—you need either a personal fortune or a war chest of contributions.

The good news is that, in the United States, national elections still cannot be bought—either through illegal maneuvering or by outspending your opponents during your campaign. The bad news is that, while you can easily spend a ton of money and lose, you *must* spend a ton of money to win. (There are now some efforts afoot to change this.)

Seats at certain tables are only acquired by persistent, assertive, ongoing pressure—and sometimes "ongoing" can mean years or decades.

In 1906, with the stroke of a pen, President Teddy Roosevelt took the Blue Lake area of New Mexico from the Tewa Tribe and gave it to the federal government. Ostensibly, this was to protect the watershed. But to the Tewas, who had legally owned the land, their entire table and every seat at it were suddenly taken away.

The Tribe responded by relentlessly pressuring the United States Forest Service, Congress, the Supreme Court, and multiple presidents for the return of its land. For *65 years*, through many different legal challenges, public relations campaigns, and other initiatives, the Tewas pushed to get Blue Lake back.

Eventually, it worked. In 1970, after three generations of pressure, ownership of Blue Lake was returned to the Tribe.

My father often used this same technique to get what he wanted. Like the Tewa leaders, he combined civility with steady, stalwart pressure—and he would give people the sense that he would never stop or go away until he got the results he wanted. As a result, he often succeeded where others would have failed. (But he did not have the Tewas' patience, so sometimes he gave up too soon.)

Seats at certain tables will be in accessible to you because they can only be inherited, or given to members of a group to which you can never belong. Forget about those tables. Instead, strategically analyze the other possibilities that interest you.

Which tables will enable you to have the biggest positive impact—on the world, on the relevant group or cause, and on you and your family? For each table, how much time, effort, energy, and/or money will getting a seat require? For each seat, what are your chances of success? Weigh the possibilities, then choose your best option and go for it.

One final thought: sometimes it's possible to simply walk in, sit down at a table, and say, "Hello. I'm joining you." This strategy occasionally works when all other attempts to obtain a seat have failed.

Most of the time you will probably be quickly escorted to an exit. But sometimes the other folks at the table may smile and say, "Welcome. It was politically impossible for us to invite you. But now that you're here, we're happy to have you. Roll up your sleeves and dive in."

It's even possible that others at the table will sigh with relief and say, "Finally. What took you so long?"

❈ OTHER KEY LESSONS ❈

- Positions on many important nonprofit boards and councils are appointed, but also partly earned *and* partly paid for.
- Financial contributions are often more important to getting on a nonprofit board than they are to staying on it.
- Seats at certain tables are only acquired by persistent, assertive, ongoing pressure—and sometimes "ongoing" can mean years or decades.
- Strategically analyze all the potential tables that interest you. Which will enable you to have the biggest positive

impact? For each table, how much time, effort, energy, and/ or money will getting a seat require? For each seat, what are your chances of success?

- Sometimes it's possible to simply walk in, sit down at a table, and say, "Hello. I'm joining you." This strategy occasionally works when all other attempts to obtain a seat have failed.

5 Always Plan at Least Two Different Routes to the Table. Three Routes Are Better Still.

No matter how well you plan, and no matter who you get on your side, sometimes your route to the table will get blocked. It could be by design, or it could be by accident. It doesn't matter. You always need a Plan B in your back pocket, so you can pull it out and implement it when your Plan A unexpectedly falls to pieces.

If you're thinking, JB, *I don't need a Plan B, because everything in my Plan A is already signed, sealed, and delivered*, you've missed my point. You can have every signature on every dotted line, and a fire destroys the document. You can build a machine that generates clean energy for two cents per megawatt, and terrorists blow up the building it's in. You can have a firm commitment from the President of the United States, and he dies of a heart attack that night.

When I filed for candidacy for the Florida House of Representatives, I had to mail a check for the filing fee to the Florida Division of Elections in Tallahassee. This couldn't be a personal check. It had to be a check from my campaign, signed by my campaign treasurer.

Four days before the deadline to file, I mailed the required check—from the required account, with the required signature—to the Division of Elections. A day later I got a call from someone in that office, who said, "JB, we received your check. We can see that it's signed by your treasurer. It looks like it's from a campaign account. But we're not 100% sure. We need you to send us a fax saying that this particular check, for this particular amount, with this particular number, is from your campaign."

I said, "Fine. I'll send you an e-mail."

She said, "No. It has to be a fax. And we have to receive it by noon on Friday."

This was in 2016. Who in 2016 had a fax machine? Plus, I was busy with campaigning, all day, every day. I couldn't give the task to one of my young volunteers. They'd just say, "A fax? What's that?" or, "Oh, yeah, my dad had one of those. You hook it up to a VCR or a turntable, right?"

As I sat at my kitchen table, I thought, *Who in 2016 still has a fax machine?*

When the answer clicked in my brain, I laughed. The solution was literally under my feet.

I left my apartment, took the elevator to the lobby, and walked into the leasing office. I said to the woman behind the desk, "Good morning. Do you guys have a fax machine?"

"We do, JB," she said. "Not that we use it very much."

"Great. Would you be willing to fax one page to a number in Tallahassee for me?"

"Of course."

My backup plan cost me nothing and was only a minor pain. But Carlos Lacasa of Miami wasn't so lucky. He did everything right in his Plan A, but it still didn't work. His Plan B literally flamed out. Fortunately, he came up with a workable Plan C on the fly—but that plan cost him thousands of dollars.

Like me, Lacasa had filed for candidacy—in his case, for the Florida state senate. He had already filed his paperwork and paid the filing fee. That was his Plan A.

Then the Division of Elections informed him that, because it had miscalculated his filing fee, he needed to send them $43.20 more by the deadline of Friday at noon. So he shifted to Plan B. He had his campaign write a check for $43.20, and he sent it to Tallahassee via Federal Express for delivery first thing Friday morning.

That morning, shortly before dawn, a Fed Ex cargo jet began its approach into the Tallahassee airport with Lacasa's check for $43.20 on board. The plane never reached the airport. It crash-landed half a mile short of the runway.

Thankfully, its three-member crew all escaped with only minor injuries. But all of the plane's cargo went up in flames.

By the time Lacasa learned of the crash, the deadline was only a few hours away. And he was in Miami, almost 500 miles from Tallahassee.

Lacasa swallowed hard and made some quick phone calls. He found a private Lear jet for rent that could take him and a new check to Tallahassee in about an hour. He hurriedly cut the check, rushed to the airport, and climbed aboard. He delivered it to the Board of Elections office nine minutes before the deadline.

"It's the most expensive $43.20 ever," he told a reporter. "But if I hadn't done it, it would have cost us the election."

When I was at Yeshiva University, I had a pre-law professor named Michael Hecht. A few days before I and my fellow students were going to take the LSAT (the Law School Admission Test), Hecht gave us a lecture about having a Plan B. Here is what he told us:

> *Listen, everyone. You've been coming here all year, so you're very familiar with how to get here and how to navigate the campus. But when you come to campus to take the LSAT on Sunday, I want you to leave way, way early, and I want you to have at least two routes. I don't care if you live across the street from the testing hall. I still want you to have two different ways to get here.*
>
> *All of you have worked six months or more preparing for this test. When the test booklets get passed out, you need to be sitting down with a pencil in your hand. No matter what happens, with or without you, that LSAT is going to happen. Maybe there will be a fire down the block. Maybe the Gay Pride Parade will come down Amsterdam Avenue and you won't be able to get across. Maybe the President will show up and Secret Service people will cordon off 185th Street. I don't know what will happen. Probably nothing. But if you've got a Plan B, you're more likely to be present and ready when the LSAT begins.*

Now that I'm almost 50, I'd add this to the lesson Hecht taught us:

There may be times when the cost of a Plan B just isn't worth it. Maybe getting to the table via anything other than Plan A simply takes too much work, or time, or money, or planning, or patience.

If that's the case, be honest with yourself. Make a calculation about what it's worth to you to get to that particular table. If the cost is too high, then accept that fact and go find a different table.

If I had been in Carlos Lacasa's position when Plan A sprung a leak and Plan B crashed and burned, would I have rented a Lear jet? Possibly. Possibly not. But I would have made a new cost/benefit calculation—and decided if the added cost was worth it.

❧ OTHER KEY LESSONS ❧

- Avoid doing anything at the last minute. You may miss any opportunity to implement a Plan B.
- Assess the costs of any Plan B or C, and weigh them against the potential benefits. Just because something is doable doesn't mean it's worth doing.
- There's a world of difference between *impossible* and *extremely unlikely*. Extremely unlikely events actually happen. On rare occasions, they will happen to you.

6

No One Gets to the Table Without the Assistance Of Others. Be Willing to Accept Help—And to Ask For It.

I f you're driving in a strange city and get lost, no one is going to walk up to you at a red light and spontaneously offer to give you directions. But if you ask, most people will be glad to offer assistance.

No matter who you are, and what you can and can't do, there are people who can and will help you. But don't expect them to automatically come forward. Usually you'll need to ask them to help you.

For some people with disabilities, this can be a sensitive matter. Because so many able-bodied people assume that we're far less capable than we actually are, we often shy away from asking for help. We say, "I'm fine; I can do it myself." This is the right response when we genuinely *can* do it ourselves without great difficulty. But it's exactly the wrong thing to say when we can't—or when assistance would make things much easier for us.

Often people with disabilities need only a very small amount of help in order to be independent and successful in many other ways. But we're not going to get that help unless we ask.

In practice, a lot of people, disabled or otherwise, often think this way. We avoid asking others for help, no matter how much we need it or how much it can help us. We need to move beyond this avoidance. Help matters, and we need to ask for it.

Until recently, I was sometimes guilty of this myself. For years, I wouldn't let people hold doors open for me. If I was out for coffee with someone, I'd make a point of getting my own refill. But I was making a point I didn't need to make.

Eventually I realized two things. First, the person I was with never gave a damn whether I could get my own refill or not. They were simply happy to help. If I got my own refill, they were fine with it. If I asked them to get it for me, they were equally fine with that. Most would have been just as happy to get me a refill if I were 100% able-bodied.

Second, for an able-bodied person, holding a door open for someone, or getting them a coffee refill, takes almost no time or energy. It's not a sacrifice or a burden—not even a tiny one.

So, today, I'm willing to accept help when it's given freely. If you offer to hold open a door for me, I'll smile and say, "That's great. Thank you."

And if you don't, that's fine, too. But on those occasions when I *need* some help, I've learned to smile, say "Excuse me," and ask for it.

That said, there will be times when people assume you need help, and may rush to offer it—yet you don't need it at all. This is why it's so important to first ask, "Can I help here, or is everything okay?"

Like anyone else, I fall once in a while—maybe once every few months. Partly it's because anyone can stumble on an obstacle, but sometimes it's because of my cerebral palsy. On rare occasions, without any warning, my legs suddenly give out.

When I do fall, I'm actually much less likely to hurt myself than most able-bodied people, because I learned how to fall safely when I was very young. When I fall, I automatically fall forward into a pushup position. Usually the worst that happens is that I scrape some skin off my hands.

Getting up isn't that hard, either, so long as I can reach my canes. But most able-bodied people don't realize any of this. I remember an incident at the Florida State Capitol. I was meeting with Jeff Atwater, the state's Chief Financial Officer, and his aide Cheri. We were walking down a hall when my legs suddenly gave out and I went down.

I landed in my usual pushup position. I did a quick body scan and could tell that I was fine.

But a few seconds later I was surrounded by people. They asked me, "Are you okay?" and "Do you need an ambulance?"

"I'm fine," I said. "All I need is a little room."

I got up, dusted myself off, straightened my tie, and said, "Thanks, everyone. I'm good."

The only person who hadn't rushed forward was Cheri. When I'd gone down, she had actually stepped *back*. Then she'd waited quietly until I was on my feet again.

I thought I knew exactly why, but I wanted to know for sure. So I asked her, "Hey, Cheri, what gives? How come you stepped back and didn't try to help me?"

She smiled. "My brother has cerebral palsy, like you. He sometimes falls the same way you just did. I knew you wouldn't need any help. All you needed was for people to get out of your way."

That confirmed my guess. "Good move," I said. "Thank you."

Some months back, I went out for dinner with my friend Sabrina at a fancy restaurant in Miami. Sabrina is young, gorgeous, very sharp, and a quadriplegic.

We were waiting in line to get to the hostess table and put in our names. I was standing with my two canes, and Sabrina sat in front of me in her wheelchair.

Suddenly, two very handsome young men appeared, cut directly in front of Sabrina, and stood there, claiming that place in the line. They didn't look at either of us and acted as if we didn't exist.

This struck me as both very rude and very strange. It seemed to me that if Sabrina had been standing up, the young men wouldn't have butted in front of her. Instead, they would have noticed how gorgeous she was and tried to chat her up.

I said to Sabrina, "Wow, that was rude. Doesn't that bother you?"

Sabrina shook her head and said, "JB, for every jackass out there who ignores us, there are several beautiful people who will help us. Just watch throughout the night."

Eventually we reached the hostess counter and put in our names. The wait was 30 minutes, so we decided to have dessert first at a nearby Ben & Jerry's.

As we got close to the door of the ice cream shop, a huge man suddenly swept in front of us. He grabbed the door, opened it wide for us, and said, "After you, folks."

"You see?" Sabrina said when we got inside. "Keep watching. It will happen all night."

And it *did* happen all night. People held open doors for us, moved aside for us, and let us get in front of them.

Maybe you're surprised that I was surprised. But, remember, I can walk. People sometimes offer to help me, but most of the time they look me up and down and think, *Do I need to help this guy? Nah, he's getting around fine.* Then they keep going and, sometimes, give me a smile and a nod. Which, most of the time, is exactly what I want. But for someone in a wheelchair, it's a completely different situation.

⁓⁂⁓ OTHER KEY LESSONS ⁓⁂⁓

- If you can do something well and relatively easily on your own, do it yourself. If you can't, let others help you.
- When you do need help, ask for it—and graciously accept it.
- Don't expect other people to intuit what you need. Ask for what you need clearly and specifically.
- Be ready to help others when you can—if their request is reasonable and fair.
- If you're not sure whether someone needs your help, ask them.
- Sometimes the most helpful thing you can do is step back and get out of the way.
- For every person who doesn't care, there are several who do. For everyone who won't offer help, there are several who will.
- Whenever possible, make dinner reservations so you don't have to wait in line.
- Whether you're disabled or able-bodied, if you're an adult, it really is okay to eat dessert first.
- If you're single and want a partner, don't overlook the attractive person in the wheelchair.

7 Assemble a Posse Of Advocates Who Will Help You Get to the Table

One of the surprising benefits of being physically disabled is that when I do something for a good cause—especially if it's physically taxing—lots of people follow my lead. In the process, they support and inspire me as well.

Sometimes people say to me, "JB, it's not about your disability. People follow and support you because you're a high-profile guy. You're well known in the community; people like you. If you suddenly stopped walking funny and gave your canes away, people would still follow your lead."

That may be partly true. But there's also something about disabled individuals doing noble things that uniquely inspires people. I know this because I witnessed the same effect when I was in high school.

For over 40 years, an annual spring event called March to Jerusalem was held in Montreal. This was a 26-kilometer walkathon that raised money for the Bronfman Israel Experience Center. The BIEC enabled young Jewish adults to visit and experience Israel at no cost. Like most walkathons, participants collected pledges of donations for each kilometer they walked.

In high school, I participated in two Marches to Jerusalem. Each time I raised hundreds of dollars for the BIEC. I finished all 26k each time, and my long walk using two canes was written up in the Montreal newspapers. (In case you're wondering, I finished closer to the back of the pack than the front. And, yes, I was tired.)

But, more important, I also gently encouraged other people to join me. I didn't twist anyone's arm; I simply invited them. And when I did, very few said no. I believe most of them thought, *If Joseph can finish the walk with two canes—and raise money for a good cause in the process—I can certainly do my part.* Collectively, they generated far more donations than I did.

When there's a good cause involved, I like bringing everyone along with me for the ride (or the walk). Even more, I like the support and inspiration they give to me. Everybody wins. I raise money for a cause I believe in. Together, the people who join me raise even more money. We all inspire each other. And we all feel good about what we've done.

I've learned that sometimes you can bring others to the table without pushing or shoving. Simply show up, and others may want to show up as well.

And when they do, they will often help you claim—or maintain—your own place at the table.

Now let's flash forward four decades, to a similar event 1400 miles to the south.

Since 2011, Stand Among Friends at Florida Atlantic University has organized an annual run, walk, race, and parade to benefit people with disabilities, called the emb(race)®. There are two different courses: one five kilometers, the other one mile. People of all ages and abilities participate on foot, with canes, on crutches, on bicycles, on hand cycles, in wheelchairs, in racing chairs, on rollerblades, and occasionally on unicycles. Some people race to win; others push themselves but don't race; some simply meander and have fun. As with the March to Jerusalem, participants collect pledges and invite others to walk, run, ride, or roll with them. The emb(race)® is sponsored by a wide range of businesses, including Sysco, Re/Max, Evolution Fitness, Orange Theory Fitness, and dozens of others.

In February of 2017, I participated in the 5K emb(race)® using my two canes. Unlike when I walked in the Marches to Jerusalem, in this event I didn't stand out at all. Hundreds of people with a variety of disabilities walked, ran, cycled, or otherwise traveled beside me to raise money for Stand Among Friends.

I'm pleased to say that, as a middle aged and well-connected guy, I was just as able to bring other people to the table as I did when I was an ambitious and idealistic teenager. I was also able to raise a nice chunk of money for a good cause.

I need to say more about Stand Among Friends and its founder and president, Shawn Friedkin. Shawn has assembled a great posse to help talented people with disabilities take their places at a variety of professional tables. As a member of Stand Among Friends' board, I'm part of that team.

Shawn is a paraplegic. He was born able-bodied, but 20 years ago, as he was driving, someone ran a red light and smashed into him. Since then he's been in a wheelchair, paralyzed from the chest down.

Shawn realized that one of the biggest obstacles for people with disabilities is that, no matter how talented or well-trained they may be, they're not always skilled at competing for jobs. Many employers have an unconscious or conscious bias against hiring people with disabilities, so those people need to be able to show potential employers just how valuable they can be.

Stand Among Friends works with new and prospective college graduates who have disabilities to help them apply for, interview for, and land the jobs they want. SAF also helps them obtain and use assistive devices that will enable them to perform as well as, or better than, able-bodied people.

One example: Patrick was earning a bachelor's degree in computer science, while working at a low-level job that paid under $9 an hour. As he neared graduation, he began working with Stand Among Friends, which helped him find and learn to use the right adaptive device, and to pitch his skills to potential employers in the right way. When Patrick completed the SAF training program and his bachelor's degree in computer science, he landed a job with the Social Security Administration that paid $78,000 a year.

Shawn likes to say, "People with disabilities don't want a handout. They want a hand up." That hand up is what Stand Among Friends provides—and what everyone who sponsored a participant in the emb(race)® helped to support.

❧ OTHER KEY LESSONS ❧

- Many people will do the right thing—but only if you ask them to. Much of the time, if you say nothing, people will do nothing.
- Sometimes, just by showing up at an important place or event, you will encourage others to show up as well.
- Don't try to set an example. Simply do what you believe in and know is right. Without even trying, you'll automatically serve as an example—and a role model.

---

8 If Your Advocates Can't Or Won't Help You Get to the Table, Look For New Advocates

For many years, I was a Democrat. Like most Democrats, I understand the importance of social services, and the role that government needs to play in providing them.

But I also know that all government services need to be paid for—and that all budgets need to balance. Republicans understand this much better than Democrats.

So I'm a moderate who leans in both directions, but who mostly leans in the direction of reason.

I don't believe in writing liberal or conservative laws. I believe in writing sensible ones. The driving force behind any law should be necessity, not ideology. When legislators address genuine human needs, they almost always create good laws. But when they advance a purely ideological agenda, they tend to create bad ones. Sometimes very bad ones.

As you know, in 2014 I decided to run for the state senate of Florida. Because I'm a moderate, I very briefly considered running in the Democratic primary. But while I have many Democratic friends—including four U.S. Congressmen—I knew that the Florida Democratic machine would have no interest in me, since it already controlled the seat, and the incumbent was running for re-election. The last thing the Democrats wanted was a challenge from inside the party. Even though there is plenty in the Democratic Party platform that I agree with—such as a concern for families' health and success**—the Dems simply were not going to welcome me to the ballot. (BTW, there are also quite a few things in the Democratic platform that I disagree with.)

I'm well aware that the Republican Party would have responded in exactly the same way if I had wanted to challenge its own incumbent in a primary. It's how our political process works.

Given this situation, I looked for some new advocates in the Republican Party. There is plenty in the Republican platform that I agree with—such as a concern for businesses' health and success—so I knew I would feel equally at home there. (I of course disagree with some items in the Republican platform as well.)

The Republicans welcomed me with open arms—up to a point. As you've seen, the Republican establishment didn't say, "Buzz off." Nor did they say, "Great! You're our guy." What they did say was, "Not now, JB We're happy to have you run for office, and we're happy to get behind you—but not for *this* seat in *this* election. We'll help you get to the table, but not right now, and not in this particular way."

---

* Why do people think we can't have healthy, successful families *and* healthy, successful businesses? Of course we can. The two are complements, not opposites, and I'm a huge supporter of both.

That was a hell of a better opportunity than the Democrats could offer me.

Sometimes even everyday situations require you to look for new advocates.

A couple of years ago, I wanted to surprise my significant other with 21 bouquets of flowers. (The number 21 had great significance for both of us.) So I called a local flower shop and spoke to a polite teenaged clerk. He took my order and quoted me a price. I okayed it and said, "I'd like them delivered this Sunday."

There was a second or two of silence on the line. Then the clerk said, "I'm sorry, sir. We can deliver them first thing Monday morning. We don't deliver on Sundays."

"You do now," I said politely. "I just ordered 210 flowers."

"I appreciate that, sir," he said. "But we're closed on Sundays."

The young man was pleasant and friendly, but he was obviously not my advocate.

I'd been a business owner long enough to know what to do. I said, "Would you put your boss on the phone, please?"

He did. An equally pleasant woman said, "This is Bernice, one of the owners. Can I help you?"

"You can. I just ordered 210 flowers, to be delivered to an address here in town.

You'll see that the order is for about $500. But I need them delivered this Sunday. You can do that, can't you?"

The practical and gracious owner said, "Of course."

❖ OTHER KEY LESSONS ❖

- When someone offers to help you get to the table—but on their terms and timeline, not yours—seriously consider that offer.

- Almost everyone who says "no" answers to someone who has the power to say "yes."

- Sometimes even everyday situations require you to look for new advocates.

- When you're told that something can't be done or isn't allowed, don't give up and go away. Instead, look for a way to bend, change, remove, or circumvent the rule.

- When you want something done, the right question is not, "Can you do X?" It's "I need you to do X," or "You can do X, can't you?"

9 When Necessary, Turn Your Opponents Into Advocates

Most people go to church or synagogue for the religious services—what I sometimes call "the big weekend show." But at most houses of worship, there are hundreds of other people who show up regularly during the week. These folks use the facility as a social service center.

I wrote my master's thesis on the subject on synagogues as social service centers. As part of my research and training, I spent a year at a synagogue on the Upper West Side of Manhattan. From the fall of 1994 to the spring of 1995, I was there Mondays, Wednesdays, and Fridays (as well as many Friday nights and Saturday mornings). My role was a combination of social worker, intern, and volunteer.

On my very first visit to the synagogue, I saw that it had a problem: its sanctuary and rest rooms weren't accessible for wheelchairs.

This was somewhat understandable. The building had been constructed in the late 1800s, in a gothic style with multiple stairways. I could see that making it handicapped accessible wouldn't be cheap—though it wouldn't be prohibitively expensive, either.

Since I'm fine with stairs, none of this affected me personally. But I knew that, as a social worker in training, I needed to advocate for other people with disabilities.

Besides, as part of my master's degree, I had to complete what was called a practice class; I had to create a significant positive change in some public venue, location, or context.

So I decided that, as part of my work at the synagogue, I would convince its board to make the sanctuary and at least one rest room handicapped accessible.

By 1994, the Americans with Disabilities Act had already been law for several years. But it didn't apply to religious institutions, for reasons I'll discuss later in this chapter. Still, some houses of worship in Manhattan had already become handicapped accessible, so I knew that I wasn't proposing anything radical or strange.

I started by making my case to the senior rabbi. He got on board immediately and asked, "How can I help?"

But I didn't go to the board just yet. I knew that they viewed me as a volunteer who would not likely stay beyond May. This meant that if I pitched an idea to them, they could simply discuss it for a few months until they'd run out the clock. Then I'd be gone and they wouldn't have to deal with me and my issue any more. I wanted to avoid that scenario.

So, instead, I said to the senior rabbi, "We need to create a social service committee made up mostly of dues-paying members, so that this initiative comes from within the congregation. I'll just be the consultant who provides the expertise."

The rabbi said, "Good," and he gave me the names of half a dozen people who he felt would want to be part of a social service committee.

At the top of the list was a woman named Lisa. "She's one of the most active people in the synagogue community," he told me. "Call her."

I did. I soon learned that she had already started a prison pen pal program and an adopt-a-grandparent program. She asked me why I had called her. I said, "It seems odd to me that if there's a bar mitzvah or a High Holy Day service, someone in a wheelchair has to be carried in, and if they need to go to the bathroom, they have to wait until they get home." She understood immediately, and, together, we began assembling a social service committee.

Once the committee had solidified, we took a proposal to the synagogue's board.

The board's first response was—somewhat predictably—not very positive. "it's too expensive," they said, "and we don't have a budget for it. Anyway, not many people are going to need it. Few disabled people come here."

I pointed out that this was precisely *because* they couldn't get in the door or use the bathroom on their own.

As we talked, it became clear that the board wasn't against accessibility. They didn't specifically *want* to exclude disabled people from the synagogue. So, eventually, we were able to reframe the question from "Should we make the synagogue handicapped accessible?" to "How can we fund such an effort and make it happen?"

That was a turning point. It enabled Lisa and the committee and I to begin to talk with congregants about the idea. Slowly and surely, it resonated with people, and we began to create a way forward.

We got especially strong support from women in the congregation, for an entirely unexpected reason. The existing women's rest rooms were often crowded, and there weren't enough stalls. Understandably, this was an ongoing source of annoyance. Adding a unisex handicapped rest room meant not just accommodating disabled people; it also meant *adding another rest room.*

Our committee of course leveraged this, and soon most of the women in the congregation were our firm advocates.

That tipped the scales in our favor. No one wanted to take a position against Lisa, me, the social service committee, people with disabilities in general, *and* the women of the congregation.

By the end of 1994, our plan was approved—and by the time my internship ended, anyone in a wheelchair could easily, on their own, enter or leave the building, pray, and make a trip to the rest room.

Something else happened by the end of 1994: Lisa and I had begun dating. Before my internship ended we were engaged, and we got married in the summer of 1995.

Most people don't realize it, but the elder President George Bush—a moderate Republican—was a driving force behind the Americans with Disabilities Act. The ADA required businesses, employers, and people in general to treat those of us with disabilities equally.

Bush had personal motives for pushing for the passage of this law: he had a grandchild with a serious disability. He knew that unless something was done to reduce the bias against handicapped people, nobody was going to hire his grandson when he grew up.

Until Bush became a grandfather, he didn't think much about the subject. But once it affected him personally, it became part of his mission in life. (Bush spoke about this at a 20th anniversary celebration of the ADA in 2010.)

Have you noticed that when elected officials have personal experience with an issue, they tend to take a sensible position on it—and when they don't, they often tend toward senselessness? Like it or not, this is how things often work.

And not just among elected officials. Stanford University became handicapped accessible many years before most other U.S. universities—not because its leaders were exceptionally wise and forward thinking, but because its president had a family member who was a paraplegic.

In part because of his own experience with his grandson, President Bush knew that unless Americans were forced by law to be fair to people with disabilities, they simply wouldn't. I believe it was an act of genius and courage for Bush to set aside his hopes and ideology and say to America, in essence, "Friends, I don't trust you on this. You need to do the right thing, and in this case the only way that will happen is if we pass a national law that requires you to. So that's what I'm going to push for."

But Bush wasn't an autocrat. He didn't try to write the law himself. Instead, he called a meeting with every state attorney general in the nation and said, "We need equality and fairness for people with disabilities. I want all of you to work together to write a law that makes sense."

They did, and Congress passed it in 1990. It was signed into law on July 26 of that year.

I learned about the passage of the ADA the following morning, while I was vacationing in Barcelona with my father, mother, and sister. We were having breakfast together at a café. Most of us chatted while my father silently read the *International Herald Tribune*.

Suddenly my father said, "Wow. This is amazing. Everybody, stop for a moment. Listen to what the USA just did." Then he read to us parts of the *Herald Tribune* article, which was about the passage of the ADA. He looked at me and said, "Joseph, this law is revolutionary. You have to become a U.S. citizen."

That actually wasn't much of a stretch for me. I was already living in New York and attending Yeshiva University. And I was very excited about the passage of the ADA. For all that Canada had done for me when I was a child, it had no national law guaranteeing equal rights to people with disabilities. (I applied for U.S. citizenship in 1995, when I got married, and became a joint American/Canadian citizen in 2000.)

I admit that I was skeptical at first about how well the ADA would work in practice. Would people follow it or ignore it? Would it create a backlash against people with disabilities? Would it create resentment or anger or competition? I decided to find out for myself.

In 1991, shortly after the ADA went into effect, I spent my spring break driving from New York to Florida and back. Whenever I stopped at any rest room, restaurant, gas station, or motel—and, in all, I must have stopped at dozens—I deliberately checked to see if it was handicapped accessible.

Every single one was.

Better still, when I thanked people for their fairness and consideration, not a single one grumbled. No one said, "You disabled people don't deserve this." No one looked at me funny and said, "Yeah, well, enjoy it, cripple." Everyone smiled—or else shrugged, like it was no big deal—and they all said, "Of course. It's the law." (One hippie said, "Hey, man, it's the law. Gotta do what Uncle Sam says.")

It was a great spring break. I was secure in the knowledge that whatever public place I went to—whether it was in Seattle, Sacramento, or Saratoga Springs—I'd be able to use the bathroom, get a drink of water, enjoy a meal in a restaurant, or make my way to a hotel room.

This was deeply empowering for those of us with disabilities. The law had our backs. Because of the ADA, our former opponents had become our advocates.

Even in 2017, I can't assume that everything in Canada will be handicapped accessible. But if it's a public facility in the United States, I can trust that it will be. In the 25 years since the passage of the ADA, that trust has not been violated.

Thank you, America. Thank you, Congress. Thank you, George H.W. Bush.

I was so impressed by the ADA that, in 1991, I wrote an op ed piece about it for the *Montreal Gazette*. It took the form of a letter to then-Prime Minister Brian Mulroney. In essence, I asked the Prime Minister, "Why is it that Canada has a national strategy for the integration of disabled people, but no actual laws to enforce that strategy?" I insisted that Canada didn't need a strategy; it needed a law, like the ADA in America, which was a huge, unqualified success.

As of this writing, in 2017, Canada still has no such law.

There's one other aspect of the Americans with Disabilities Act that was extremely wise. Its creators specifically carved out an exception for religious institutions—churches, synagogues, mosques, meditation centers, church camps, seminaries, and so on.

Why was this so wise? Because making facilities handicapped accessible was and is expensive.

The folks who wrote the law understood that if—and only if— religious institutions were exempt from the law, they would strongly support it, on ethical (and sometimes religious) grounds. That turned out to be exactly what happened.

They also understood that if religious organizations were forced to comply with the ADA, they would push back against it big time. Churches around the country would align themselves against disabled people. Did the U.S. government really want to pick a fight with (for example) the Catholic Church? Realistically, was it going to sue the Pope? The country would be torn apart. People with disabilities would be seriously pissed, and the ADA would have become a recipe for chaos and misery.

Instead, the religious exemption wound up making the law stronger, not weaker, because it accommodated the one group of organizations that had the power to sabotage it and organize against it.

But, of course, as the years passed, many religious facilities became handicapped accessible anyway—not because they had to, but because it was the right thing to do. Churches, mosques, synagogues, and so on wanted to be as accessible as the hotel, restaurant, and gas station down the street. They also didn't want to be in the position of saying to the world, "The ADA is a great law. People with disabilities should be treated equally—by everyone except us. But we're not interested in accommodating them."

The people who wrote the ADA clearly understood that this was what would happen. They created a nuanced law that worked brilliantly.

But not perfectly—as I discovered to my disappointment in 2015.

I was in downtown Boston, at a market complex called Quincy Market. I wanted to go upstairs, so I followed a sign that pointed to the elevator and to the handicapped-accessible rest room. But the elevator wasn't working—and the handicapped rest room was upstairs.

For me, this wasn't a problem, since I can handle stairs. But for someone in a wheelchair, everything above the first floor would have been inaccessible.

I called security and asked about the elevator. The man who answered said, "Yeah, it was working yesterday. Today's Sunday, so they'll probably fix it tomorrow."

Very politely, I told him, "I know this isn't your fault. But your bosses need to know that when there's no access for disabled people, it's a violation of federal law."

It would have been one thing if the elevator had just broken a few minutes earlier and a repair crew was on its way over. Everyone understands that you need professionals to fix an elevator, and that they need time to get there. But letting a broken elevator sit for a day or two is thoughtless, unfair, and illegal.

If Stephen Hawking, or Christopher Reeve, or Congressman Jim Langevin had shown up that afternoon, he would have been out of luck. (This isn't as far-fetched as it sounds. Langevin lives less than an hour away by train, so he very well could have visited that day.)

Think of it this way. If the electricity in the whole complex had gone out, would management have said, "You know what? It's Sunday morning. We don't need to get current flowing again until Monday"? Of course not.

This incident took place only a few days after I'd written most of this chapter. I'd just noted, with great appreciation, how fortunate it is for us disabled people that we have access to a rest room in any public facility in the United States.

It turns out that there are still occasional exceptions.

※ OTHER KEY LESSONS ※

- Doing the right thing is often expensive. But that's almost never a good reason to avoid doing it.
- To get people on your side, frame your ideas as investments or opportunities rather than as costs.
- If you want to talk Jill into assisting Jack, focus heavily on the potential benefits for Jill.
- When possible and practical, help people see for themselves the wisdom of doing the right thing.
- When this isn't possible or practical, work to pass a law that forces them to do the right thing.
- Don't just assign tasks. Encourage people to complete them in a way—and toward an outcome—that makes sense.
- When people do something wise or sensible or courageous, thank everyone involved for their efforts.
- When a person, group, or institution takes a big leap forward, encourage—or challenge—their counterparts to do the same.
- Understand who your biggest opponents are likely to be. Then design a strategy that either works around them, gets them on your side, or both.

10

Sometimes the Fastest Route to the Table Is Asking the Right Questions

I n 2016, I got a call from the president of the national Private Care Association. He'd recently spoken to the mother of a child who had been denied Medicaid benefits, and he wondered if I could help her in some way. I said, "Have her call me. If there's something I can do, I will."

Soon she called. Her name was Jenny, and she was the wife of a popular minister in Florida. She and her husband had adopted their son years earlier, when he was three. They quickly discovered that for those first three years of his life, he had received almost no love or nurturing. As a result, he had what social workers and psychologists call *reactive attachment disorder*. In ordinary language, it meant that he refused to bond with anyone or accept love from anyone. As a result, he was very angry, very destructive, and often uncontrollable.

But reactive attachment disorder can be treated—and, over time, children can and do heal from it.

Unfortunately, treatment for such a serious condition isn't quick, easy, or inexpensive, so Jenny and her husband asked Medicaid to cover the costs. Medicaid said no, claiming that the treatment was experimental and that there was no proof that it worked.

Does this sound familiar? If so, it's because it's the same dodge private insurance companies have sometimes used to deny coverage to their clients. (To be fair, some treatments *don't* work, or genuinely *are* still in the experimental stage. It's perfectly reasonable for both public and private insurers to deny claims for such treatments. But it's not reasonable to use these concepts as pretexts to deny legitimate claims.)

Jenny, was understandably angry and upset about the denial. She had filed an appeal inside Medicaid, and she was scheduled to make her case before an administrative judge in a Florida state court in a few weeks. The judge would then decide one of two things: 1) that Jenny's appeal was spurious, and she would have to respect Medicaid's original decision, or 2) that Jenny's appeal was legitimate, so she had the right to sue Medicaid in civil court.

It seemed to me that Medicaid had denied the family's claim in bad faith. I suspected that Medicaid might have some kind of bias— either against the particular form of treatment or against treating severe detachment disorder at all.

Here is what I told Jenny:

"When you go to the hearing, you won't be the only person making a case. The person who said no to providing coverage for your son will be there, too. They might be a physician, or a Medicaid claims examiner, or some other bureaucrat. Probably it will be a physician. Whoever it is, I want you to speak to them directly, and ask them these two questions:

"First: how many times have you examined or met with my son?

"Second: how, exactly, did you arrive at your decision to deny the claim?"

I was able to be so prescriptive because I already knew what the Medicaid examiner's answers would be.

At the hearing, Jenny followed my instructions perfectly. She asked the Medicaid bureaucrat—who was indeed a physician—how many times he had examined or met with her son. He answered, "Never. I've never met him."

Jenny said, "I see. And how did you arrive at your decision to deny our claim?"

The doctor launched into an explanation of protocols, regulations, eligibility, and other administrative blather, none of which involved an actual human being who was ill, who was suffering, and who needed treatment.

As the doctor droned on, the judge became more and more impatient. She seemed astounded that he had never met Jenny's son.

As soon as the doctor finished talking, the judge said to Jenny, "How did you know to ask these questions?"

Jenny said, "I have a friend who's an advocate."

"Uh huh," the judge said. "Is he a lawyer?"

"No. He's running for state legislature."

The judge sat back in her chair. "I hope he wins," she said. "We need more people like him in Tallahassee."

The judge delivered her decision a few weeks later: Jenny and her husband were entitled to sue Medicaid in civil court for a bad-faith denial of their claim.

The judge's ruling came down on July 9, 2016 at 10:00 am. At 8:00 p.m. that same day, I got an e-mail from Jenny. She told me that Medicaid had agreed to cover all the expenses for her son's treatment— past, present, and future.

❧ OTHER KEY LESSONS ❧

- An explanation that is 100% sensible and legitimate in some situations may be entirely bogus in others.
- When a rationale fails to take into account its effects on living, breathing human beings, that rationale is almost always flawed.
- Asking good questions is always a powerful strategy.

11

Anticipate the Ways In Which People May Try to Keep You Away From the Table. Then Outthink and Outplan Them.

Like most teenagers, I wanted to get my driver's license as quickly as possible. In Montreal in the 1980s, that meant enrolling in and completing a driver education program as soon as I turned 16.

I knew I'd be able to drive. I'd watched my parents do it for years. But my mother and cousins were very concerned about me driving a regular car. They feared that, because of my cerebral palsy, I wouldn't be able to brake quickly enough in an emergency. They wanted me to complete driver ed using a car for the disabled—one with hand controls for braking and accelerating.

I already knew that I didn't need these. I told my mom and my cousins, "I'll be able to drive just fine. Leave me alone." But some of my relatives continued to object.

This wasn't a matter of pride; I was simply thinking ahead. I knew that, as an adult, I might sometimes need to rent a car, and I didn't want to face a lifetime of limited transportation options. (Remember, this was decades before anyone even conceived of Uber.)

One night my father asked me, point blank, "Joseph, can you drive a car without special accommodations?"

I said, "Yes."

My father simply nodded and said, "Okay, then."

The next day he went to Sears and came home with a mannequin and a stopwatch. To this day I have no idea how he convinced the people at Sears to sell him one of their mannequins. But somehow he did.

The next day, after school, my dad and I drove out to a vacant part of a mall parking lot. The mannequin, the stopwatch, and my father's video camera were in the back seat. He got out, unloaded everything, and said, "Okay, Joseph, drive around, pass me every 30 seconds or so, and brake whenever you need to."

I did as he asked. Most of the time when I passed my father, he simply followed me with his camera. But occasionally, as I drove up, he hurled the mannequin in front of the car. I hit the brakes, and each time stopped quickly and safely. We practiced this for about 15 minutes.

We went back to the mall again two days later and practiced for another 15 minutes. Again, I had no problem stopping in time.

The following morning my father and I went to a nearby driving school, and I signed up for the standard driver ed program. The man behind the counter looked at me and said, "So, Joseph, we're going to need to get you a car with hand controls."

My father smiled and said, "That won't be necessary." He handed the man a videotape. "Here, play this tape. It runs about three minutes."

The man gave my father a strange look, but he stood up and said, "Sure. Follow me."

We went into a cubicle that had a video player. He popped in the tape, which contained six different brief, identical incidents. Each one began with a view of an empty parking lot. Then, suddenly, a mannequin flew into view and landed on the pavement. Two seconds later, the front end of a car appeared and came to a full, safe stop a foot or two in front of the limp figure.

When the video ended, my father handed the man a sheet of paper. "I used a stopwatch to check Joseph's braking times. Here's a complete record of those times."

By now the man was smiling, and perhaps trying to keep from laughing. "Joseph," he said to me, "I can see that you won't need any special accommodation."

With his simple but brilliant strategy, my father did several things at once. He challenged me to prove that what I said about my abilities was true. He trained me to make sure that my claim *became* true. And he provided tangible proof to any and all doubters (including my mother and cousins) that my claim *was* true. It was a perfect preemptive strike that immediately swept aside any possible objection.

Thanks, Dad.

❀ OTHER KEY LESSONS ❀

- Think twice—and perhaps three times—before choosing an option that makes things easier today, but more difficult in the long run.
- Give people the chance to prove you wrong. When they do, accept the results graciously.
- Sometimes the best thing to do is *help* them prove you wrong.
- If you see something you want but it's not for sale, offer to buy it anyway. Sometimes you'll get lucky.
- Ninety percent of the time, tangible proof trumps even the best argument.

12

Be Wary When You're Invited to Sit a Table That Doesn't Interest You. Be Warier Still When People Pressure Or Encourage You to Sit There.

B y the time I was five years old, I had done thousands of hours of physical therapy. In addition to the PT provided by the provincial government, my parents arranged for a private physical therapist—a pleasant, skilled woman named Jane Livery—to come to our home.

Because of the PT, I slowly gained more and more control over my legs. But at age five, I wasn't yet able to walk on my own, even with two canes. When I went somewhere with a member of my family, I would walk with one of them holding me up. Sometimes my father or mother would carry me. Although this worked reasonably well, I yearned for the day when I would be able to walk without human assistance, with nothing more than a couple of canes.

One day soon after my fifth birthday, I watched from our living room window as Jane, my physical therapist, parked her hatchback in our driveway. Instead of walking straight to our door, she opened the back of her car and removed a wheelchair. A sick feeling spread through my gut as she wheeled it to our door and rang the doorbell.

My mother met Jane at the door and welcomed her in. I went straight up to her and said firmly, "Jane, I'm not using that chair."

Jane smiled at me. "Joseph, no one is going to make you use this chair. I just brought it over so you could try it out for a few days. If you like it, it's yours to keep. If you don't, I'll take it back."

"I already don't like it," I said. "I'm not getting into it. Not now. Not ever. Put it back in your car."

Jane and my mother looked at each other. Jane said to me, "Joseph, you're going to need to get around—"

I interrupted her. "I get it. I'm going to need to figure out how to walk on my own with canes. I can do that. I *will* do that. Now, put it back."

For a moment, everyone froze. Then Jane smiled again. "All right, Joseph," she said, "back it goes." She and the chair went out the door again.

When she returned a few minutes later, she said to me, "Joseph, your biggest job now is to learn to walk on your own."

I said, "I'm ready."

For the next two years, that was our goal. And in my seventh year, with Jane's help, I got there.

For the past four decades, with the help of two canes, I've walked more or less everywhere else that able-bodied people walk, including multiple walkathons and the Miami Marathon.

To my parents' credit, neither of them tried to talk me out of my decision. They never said, even once, "Joseph, why don't you just try it?" We didn't even discuss the subject. From the moment I sent Jane back outside with the chair, my mother and father considered the issue settled.

The wheelchair Jane brought into our home for three minutes turned out to be an enormous inspiration. It was a vivid image of what my life would be like if I didn't learn to walk under my own power.

From the time I could first talk, if I didn't want something I would say no—and stick to my guns.

Around the time I learned to walk on my own, my parents urged me to take piano lessons. They figured that, if I was good at it, I could play piano for a living. It was a career that I could build sitting down. At the time, I had no idea whether I would like the piano or not, but I figured there was no harm in trying it.

So, for six months, I practiced the piano, and took lessons in the home of a women from our neighborhood. She was friendly enough, and she played the piano well, but we had religious and philosophical differences.

She was a devout Catholic, and her house was full of images of Jesus, especially Jesus on the cross. These didn't bother me; in fact, I thought they were visually cool. What bothered me was what she told me at almost every lesson. She'd say, "Joseph, let me share something with you. If only you'll let Jesus into your heart, he can cure you. Wouldn't you like that?"

Each week I'd respond the same way: "But I don't need to be cured. I'm not sick. I just walk funny."

Eventually I told my parents about these repeated conversations, and they said, "Let's find you a different teacher."

They did, and for the next six months a new teacher came to our home to teach me. He never mentioned Jesus or told me I needed healing. I liked him fine.

But after a year of lessons, it was clear that the piano didn't appeal to me. So I told my parents, "The piano isn't for me. I don't want to take any more lessons."

My parents knew from experience that when I said no to something, I meant it. So—God bless them—they didn't try to change my mind. My father simply said, without any rancor, "Joseph, you'll regret it." To which I said, "No, I won't."

That was the end of my future career as a pianist. And, FYI, to this day I've never regretted my decision.

❋ OTHER KEY LESSONS ❋

- When your gut tells you that something feels wrong, pay attention to it.
- When you're sure that your answer is *no,* say so firmly. Don't equivocate, don't compromise, and don't try to appease anyone.
- When someone else is genuinely sure that their own answer is *no,* accept that answer graciously.
- Sometimes the dread of what you don't want can be as inspiring as the hope of what you do want.
- When someone tells you that you'll regret what you're about to do, they're only guessing—and they may well be wrong.

---

13 Remember That Your Time and Opportunities For Getting a Place at the Table Are Limited

My father David was my best friend, and an utterly unique human being.

On the most important of Jewish holidays, Yom Kippur, the Day of Atonement, Jews around the world pray for forgiveness of our sins. Each year, my father said those prayers like the rest of us, but he really didn't need to. He didn't wait for Yom Kippur; if he wronged someone, he'd ask for their forgiveness immediately, right then and there. He understood that if he put off making things right, he might not get the chance later.

He was very tolerant, very kind. He routinely practiced social justice—what we Jews call *tikkun olam*, healing the world. But he could also be very assertive and tenacious, which made him the perfect advocate.

My father taught me that education is freedom—that as long as I had an education, I would always be successful. That turned out to be 100% true for me, both financially and otherwise—though I've also learned not to let myself be hemmed in by other people's definitions of success.

My dad wasn't political. He wasn't an intellectual, although he was very bright. He was a merchant: he sold draperies for a living. But most of the Montreal Jewish community knew, liked, and respected my dad.

In December of 2000, when my father was 65, he lay down to take a nap one afternoon, feeling normal and healthy, and didn't wake up. His heart just stopped.

A thousand people showed up at his funeral.

The Talmud—the most important book of Jewish law—tells us that only the righteous die on the Sabbath. My family was deeply shocked that he died—but not at all surprised that he died on Shabbat.

For some years afterward, I had a huge beef with God. I didn't lose my faith or want to stop being Jewish. But for a long time, when I would pray, I'd often add, "You know what, God? You're an asshole. You took my father when he was young and healthy." To this day I don't regret the insults; God can obviously handle them, and I needed to vent. While we humans need to treat each other with great respect, there's nothing in the Torah or the Talmud that says, "Your Creator—the Creator of time and space, life and death—never call Him an asshole."

My father did a lot of wonderful things in his life. It hurts that he didn't live long enough to do many more. But because he was so conscious of making things right as quickly as possible, and of seizing opportunities when they arose, he left very few moral loose ends when he died.

In 2002, in my dad's memory, I created the David Bensmihen Foundation, an educational foundation that pays for the education of kids whose families can't afford the tuition. Donations to the fund turn into tuition checks to Jewish day schools and academies. In fact, 10% of all profits from this book go to that foundation.

❧ OTHER KEY LESSONS ❧

- When you're angry or upset, it's okay to vent to God.
- Education is freedom. If you've got a good education, you'll always have a path to success.
- Life is fleeting. You, or I, or any human being can die at any time. Live wisely now, because, for any of us, there may literally be no tomorrow.
- When you wrong someone, don't wait. Ask for their forgiveness at the first available opportunity.
- Don't let others define success for you.
- You don't need to be political or intellectual to do the right thing—or to have a profound and positive effect on others.

---

14 Sometimes the Best Thing to Do Is Build Your Own Table

I have a master's degree in social work with a focus in community organization. I was trained to be an advocate for individuals, groups, neighborhoods, and communities. In 1996, shortly after getting my master's degree, I became a social worker for the city of Deerfield Beach, Florida, a suburb of Fort Lauderdale.

My job was to administer the social service component of the city's Northeast Focal Point Senior Center. It was a place where seniors could go for companionship, activities, counseling, and a hot midday meal, all at no charge. I also led group therapy sessions and counseled people one-to-one.

Almost all of the people who came to Focal Point were pleasant, but I quickly learned that they fell into two very different groups.

The first group, most of whom were poor, came regularly and spent much of the day there. Five days a week, they would get picked up in the morning by a van, dropped off at the center by 8:30, and taken home again in late afternoon. I brought in speakers and entertainment for these folks, who were passive recipients of Focal Point's services.

The second group was both very selective and very engaged. They usually drove to the center for a very specific purpose—a support group meeting, a one-to-one counseling appointment, a blood pressure check, etc. Often they showed up to meet with me because their rabbi or minister or priest or doctor urged them to.

I was popular with the seniors who came to the center; I got along fine with my co-workers and superiors; and I liked the work. It also paid pretty well, at least by the standards of a man in his twenties.

In fact, if nothing had shaken me loose from the place, I might still be a social worker there today. But one day, after I'd worked at Focal Point for six months—with no warning or explanation—the city of Deerfield Beach gave me the boot. The only thing I was told was, "You're not a good fit."

To this day I don't know how the decision was made, why it was made, or who made it. It was basically, "Clean out your desk. You're out of here. And that's all we're telling you."

At first I was in shock. Then I was hurt and upset. Then I wondered what would happen to my clients. Would the city leave them in the lurch, or would my replacement be knowledgeable, caring, and client-focused?

Then I brushed myself off, got out my canes, said a few goodbyes, and left my office for the last time.

For a short time, I felt deeply embarrassed, as if I'd failed somehow—though I had no idea how. So I got over my embarrassment.

During the next two weeks, some of my clients called me at home. (This was in the days when very few people had cell phones.) They said things like, "I can't believe you left; I really liked you. I'll miss you."

That was gratifying, but I was still out of a job.

I also understood that the same thing could happen again as long as I was an employee in the state of Florida. This is because Florida is an "at will" state. This means that any employer can let go of any employee at any time. It doesn't need to explain why; it doesn't even need to have a reason. In fact, as I later learned, to avoid potential liability and legal challenges, many employers *deliberately* provide little or no reason when they let people go.

It turns out that the less an employee knows about why they're being let go, the less risk of legal action the employer faces. This puts everyone in a difficult situation. There are times when a boss would like to say to their employee, "It really hurts me to have to let you go, because your performance has always been excellent. But we need to cut a big chunk of our payroll, and we just can't afford you any longer." But instead, to protect the organization, they send a bland e-mail that says, in essence, "Hand over your keys and get out of here."

To her credit, my wife Lisa didn't say, "Well, JB, that stinks, but suck it up and find a new job." Instead, she said, "Don't worry. You'll find something else."

At the time, Lisa was working for a company called Home Heath Corporation of America. She had earned an MBA, and was handling contracts for the corporate vice president. I didn't know a lot about HHCA, but I knew that it sent nurses to people's homes to care for the elderly, the disabled, and the sick.

Lisa mentioned to her boss that I had been let go from my social worker job. Her boss said, "He's a social worker? Does he speak Spanish, by any chance? We need another social worker—one who speaks Spanish. Lisa explained that I speak fluent English and

Spanish, plus passable Hebrew and French. He said, "I'd like to meet with your husband."

Soon I had a new job as a social worker—but this time, instead of people coming to me, I went to them. I visited people in their homes in the city of Belle Glade, and one of my main tasks was to make sure that they were receiving all the care and services they needed.

This required me to build good rapport with all of them, most of whom were elderly. Often, it meant informing them about what services and opportunities were available to them. This was especially important, since a third of my clients had HIV/AIDS, and most did not speak fluent English. It also meant signing up people for Medicaid so that HHCA could get paid for home care services it provided.

For the next 14 months, Lisa and I worked for Home Health Corporation of America, taking careful note of how it functioned, how it served its clients, and how it made a profit. Then, outfitted with this knowledge, we said to each other, "Maybe we can do better on our own."

While working at HHCA, we'd discovered a niche in our health care system that desperately needed filling. Things are different—and saner—now, but back then, if you were on Medicare, and you didn't have a nurse or physical therapist assigned to visit you, then Medicare wouldn't pay to have a social worker visit you. That meant people weren't getting many of the services they needed and were entitled to, because they were clueless about the system and had no advocate to assist them. Plus, if you didn't speak English, or were old or frail, you simply wouldn't be able to advocate for yourself.

So when a doctor would say to HHCA, "Send a social worker over to Mrs. Krebs' apartment," HHCA would say, "I'm sorry, but we can't. Medicare won't pay for it unless a nurse or PT is also visiting." As a result, the doctor was unhappy; the client was unhappy; and HHCA was unhappy. Meanwhile, whatever problem had created the need for a social worker would go unaddressed.

Lisa and I thought through the situation and said to the folks at HHCA, "This is an opportunity for all of us. JB can serve as an independent visiting social worker. Instead of saying to people, 'No, sorry, we can't send a social worker, because Medicare won't pay for it,' we're offering you the chance to say, 'Sure, we'll be happy to send someone. Medicare doesn't cover it, though, so you'll be billed $50 for the visit. Is that all right?' Most people will have no trouble with the fee, and instead of upset clients, you'll have grateful ones."

HHCA said, "Sure, let's try it."

So we started our own geriatric care management company, United Elder Care Services. Lisa served as the CFO, and I was the CEO and the care manager. I also became the legal guardian of some of our clients.

The business was an almost instant success. Doctors were relieved, because patients' needs were being handled. HHCA was delighted, because we were solving one of their ongoing problems. Lisa and I earned good incomes. And if you were a middle-aged woman living in Connecticut, and you were concerned that your aging father in Florida wasn't taking his meds regularly, you were very happy to spend $50 a visit to have a social worker make sure everything was okay. Everyone was a winner.

There were some other plusses as well. We were entirely outside of the official reimbursement system, so there was very little paperwork. And there was plenty of repeat business. After I'd made a few visits to an elderly man or woman, their kids would often say to me, "Can you visit my mom or dad twice a month, or once a week?" I would say, "Sure," and that became the United Elder Care Monitoring Program.

Although we started United Elder Care Services with referrals from HHCA, it wasn't long before we were getting referrals from almost every home health agency between Miami and Palm Beach. They all had the same problem, and at the time, we were the only organization that offered a simple solution.

This turned out to be one of the best decisions of our lives. Within five years, the business had become extremely successful. Within a decade, it made the two of us millionaires.

Thank you, Deerfield Beach, for giving me the boot.

❧ OTHER KEY LESSONS ❧

- What looks at first like a disappointment or a disaster might be an opportunity.
- When a decision has a negative impact on you, there may be valid reasons for it that have nothing to do with you, your ability, or your performance. There may be equally valid reasons for deliberately keeping you in the dark about it.
- When something baffling or unfair happens, you'll naturally want to know why. But you won't always get an answer. If you don't, let go and move on.
- To build a successful enterprise, look for an unaddressed problem or an unfilled niche. Then fill it.
- If lots of people are being routinely disappointed, you have a huge potential opportunity. You can build a thriving business by finding a way to change their disappointment into satisfaction.
- If you've recently lost your job—or if you're still working for someone else—ask yourself, *Can I do better on my own?*

Part 2

ONCE YOU'RE AT THE TABLE

15

Listen Respectfully to Everyone at the Table. Debate Or Challenge Them If Necessary— But Never Ignore Them.

If you're lucky enough to live in a country like the United States or Canada—and fortunate enough to meet some of its major political leaders—don't just show up. Listen up as well. And speak up when you disagree.

In my various roles, I've met with three presidents, a vice president, countless senators and members of Congress, and a governor. I've become friends with Congressman Ted Deutch of Florida and Jim Langevin of Rhode Island. I've also advised other Members of Congress, including Eric Cantor, Patrick Murphy, Tom Rooney, and Dennis Ross. I'm a registered Republican, and most of these legislators are Democrats. It doesn't matter. What matters is that when I'm in the room with them, my first task is to listen.

My second is to ask questions. And my third is to educate the people who don't understand—and debate the ones who disagree.

Listening to someone and then debating them may piss them off. But that's okay. I've learned that if your point is sensible, that person will respect you when the debate is over, regardless of who wins.

But you'll never earn somebody's respect by not paying attention to them.

In 2014, I met and listened to then-President Obama, questioned him, and briefly debated him about an issue that I felt was important.

Unfortunately, that didn't change his thinking on the subject. He seemed to care more about ideology than practicality.

Which was a shame, because the Supreme Court of the United States had *already* settled the issue in our favor—in a 9 to 0 decision, back in 2007.

So I became part of a group that sued the Department of Labor of the United States.

At issue was what's called the Companionship Exemption to the Fair Labor Standards Act. The Fair Labor Standards Act, which was passed in 1938, says that if someone is required to work more than 40 hours per week, they need to be paid time-and-half for overtime.

This makes perfect sense if you're an assembly line worker at an auto plant, an operator at a call center, a nurse in a doctor's office, or an orderly in a hospital. For these employees, the law provides some very important protections. I'm a strong proponent of the Fair Labor Standards Act.

But there are some jobs and situations where that rule *doesn't* work—and where it isn't (and shouldn't be) applied. If you're an astronaut working at the space station, you're essentially on the job 24/7. Should you get time-and-a-half for 16 hours a day, every day? What if you own your own S corporation? Should you be forced to pay yourself time-and-a-half on the weeks you work more than 40 hours, even if your business doesn't have sufficient cash flow? What if you're caring for a disabled or elderly shut-in in their own home?

To handle these kinds of situations, some reasonable exceptions have been carved out of the law. The one we sued over is called the Companionship Exemption, which was part of an amendment to the Fair Labor Standards Act passed by Congress in 1974.

The Companionship Exemption applies to people who provide paid care and companionship in people's homes. It doesn't apply to people who work in hospitals, clinics, hospices, or other health care facilities. It also doesn't apply to people who provide home care as volunteers.

This exemption says that if you buy home care for your mother, or your father, or your sister, or yourself, the people who provide that care don't have to be paid time-and-a-half after 40 hours a week. They only need to be paid their regular hourly rate.

The Companionship Exemption recognizes that providing care for a person in their home is very different from being an employee of a hospital or clinic or hospice.

The people who wrote the Companionship Exemption thought it through very carefully, based on the realities of providing and receiving home care. Every president before Obama, beginning with Jimmy Carter, has looked at the exemption and wondered about it, and in the end left it in place and unchanged. Congress has looked at it six times—and each time agreed that changing it would hurt both caregivers and consumers. Both Republican *and* Democratic Congresses came to this conclusion.

So did the Supreme Court. Some years back, a legal challenge was made to the Companionship Exemption, and the Supreme Court heard the case in 2007. It upheld the exemption in a 9-to-0 decision. *Everyone* on the court—conservatives, liberals, and middle-of-the-road justices—agreed that the Companionship Exemption was both sensible and Constitutional. I also suspect that many of the justices had elderly parents or relatives who received home care.

So, to date, five presidents (two Democrats and three Republicans), Congress (six times), and the Supreme Court have all come to the same conclusion: don't mess with the Companionship Exemption.

Even former Senator Tom Harkin, a Democrat, who was the chair of the Senate Committee on Health, Education, Labor, and Pensions—and who initially thought the rule change was a good idea—changed his mind and opposed it once he understood its real-world ramifications.

Nevertheless, President Obama went to the Department of Labor and said, in essence, "In its current form, the Companionship Exemption isn't fair. It's fine to keep it in place for home health care workers who are directly employed by the families of the folks they care for. But we need to get rid of it for home health care workers who are employed or referred by home health care registries or agencies."

The people at DOL aren't foolish or mean. They're dedicated civil servants who were given a directive. So, in December of 2012, the Department of Labor announced that the Companionship Exemption for many home health care workers would be dropped, effective January 1, 2015.

I don't believe for a minute that President Obama was trying to shaft home health care companies, or the people who buy their services, or home care workers, or even the Supreme Court. He genuinely believed the rule change would result in more income for home health workers. He simply didn't understand that the opposite would actually happen. He also thought it was legal and ethical for his office to overrule Congress and the Supreme Court. He seemed to believe that ideology should trump reality.

This felt awfully familiar to me. Where else had I experienced powerful people who thought that way?

You know the answer to that. Remember Montreal in 1975? That was when my teachers and principal told me that, because I walked funny, I shouldn't be allowed to go to a regular school with most of the other kids.

I wasn't willing to ignore or accept the proposed rule change, so I started talking to people. Lots of people.

I convened a conference call with leaders of the National Association for Home Care and Hospice and the International Franchise Association, as well as with key people from the national chains in the home care delivery system, such as Comfort Keepers, Visiting Angels, and Home Instead.

Most of the people at the chains were Republicans, so they were mostly concerned with how the change would hurt their businesses and lower their stock prices. They wanted to get some powerful Republicans in Congress to pressure the president to reverse course.

I listened to them talk for a while. Then I said, "The only person who can get through to the president about this would be a Democrat. And the Democrat who should be speaking to him about this is a gentleman named Jim Langevin. Jim is a Democratic congressman from Rhode Island. He's also a quadriplegic—and one of our industry's customers. He gets round-the-clock assistance from people who work for him two twelve-hour shifts a day, seven days a week."

I'm a bit embarrassed to say that many of my industry colleagues laughed at me. They thought I was crazy—and they weren't willing to pay attention to one of their own industry's most influential customers. They said, "Look at his voting record! He's a liberal. He's not going to agree with us. He's going to push for time-and-a-half."

My colleagues didn't understand that this wasn't a conservative-vs.-liberal, business-vs.-workers issue. On paper, the proposed rule change might *look* to some people like a potential victory for home care workers. But in practice, the change would actually harm most of those workers—while making home care less affordable for everyone but the wealthy.

So I went to Washington and met with Jim (who, since then, has become a close friend). I explained the proposed change and its likely effects on the industry and its customers. He said, "You're right. The numbers don't add up." Then he said, "JB, do you know how hard it is to find the right caregiver? Or to keep them once you find them? This change would make the whole process far more difficult for everyone."

So Jim got on board. Not too much later, the National Association for Home Care and Hospice, and many of its members, got behind him.

I continued to connect with people—business owners, customers, policy wonks, members of Congress, and people at the White House. I listened to them, questioned them, explained things to them, and sometimes debated with them. Together, a group of us created a plan.

In February 2013, in Washington, in the Office of Management and Budget, I convened a meeting of stakeholders to discuss the proposed rule change. At this meeting were people from the Domestic Policy Department of the Office of the President; people from the Department of Labor; Congressman Jim Langevin; Jim's aide; Congressman Ted Deutch; and me. It's *extremely* unusual for members of Congress to show up at such hearings; usually they just send their staffers.

At this meeting, Jim, Ted, and I presented the relevant facts and figures, which showed that doing away with the Companionship Exemption would have precisely the opposite effect of what President Obama wanted. Rather than help caregivers, it would actually reduce their earnings. It would also make things more difficult for both caregivers *and* consumers.

Ted Deutch said something particularly relevant. The previous night, in his State of the Union address, President Obama had expressed his conviction that every American worker should earn at least $9 an hour. Ted brought this up and said, in essence, "I agree with President Obama about the $9-an-hour minimum. But in the home care industry, most caregivers are already making $9 an hour—and, in many cases, much more." Ted was 100% right about this. In the Florida counties where I have done business—Broward, Palm Beach, and Pinellas—home care workers typically earn $11-12/hour.

Ted continued: "Let's do the math. We'll look at a home care worker who provides services through a licensed and regulated provider. If they earn, say, $12 an hour, the provider typically charges clients $18 an hour. If an elderly consumer on a fixed income needs twenty hours of care per week, the weekly cost of that care is $360. If they need 40 hours, the weekly cost is $720.

"Let's look at what would happen if the Companionship Exemption were taken away. If the caregiver stays overnight to look after a client, spending 12 hours in a row with them, they would have to be paid time-and-a-half for four of those hours. Instead of $144, they'd earn $168. But, remember, the provider charges the client 150% of what the caregiver receives. So, for that twelve-hour shift, the client will have to pay $252 instead of $216. That's a $36 difference for just one half-day of care. It's more than a lot of the people in my district—especially retirees on fixed incomes—can afford."

We followed up in November at a Congressional subcommittee hearing. The hearing was called *Redefining Companion Care: Jeopardizing Access to Affordable Care for Seniors and Individuals with Disabilities.* I gave my own testimony at this hearing. If you're curious about it, Google my name and the words *Congress* and *testimony*, and you'll be able to read it in full. But here, in highly compressed form, are the key concerns I expressed:

- Many elderly or disabled people need more than 40 hours a week of care; some need more than 80 hours; some need 24/7 assistance. Currently, about 40% of the people who receive home care have to pay for it out of pocket. Yet many of those people live on fixed incomes. If the price of their care goes up dramatically, they won't be able to afford it anymore.

- About 60% of home care clients have their care paid for through long-term care insurance, which typically pays a daily maximum for that care. Right now this insurance covers most or all of the cost for a very large number of people. If time-and-a-half rules go into effect, many people who now pay little or nothing for home care will suddenly be hit with bills of hundreds of dollars per week.

- In both of these cases, people aren't going to magically find the money to pay the increased costs. Unless they're very well off, they're going to simply cut back to 40 hours of care per week (or 80, with two care providers). Often this means they'll get less care than they genuinely need, which puts them at risk for falling or other accidents.

- The Companionship Exemption allows consumers and caregivers to build close, trusting relationships. It also creates continuity of care, which is especially valuable for people with dementia or Alzheimer's. Were the new rule to be implemented, this continuity would be disrupted—e.g., a live-in caretaker, or two trusted caregivers on twelve-hour shifts, would typically be replaced with three caregivers on eight-hour shifts. This would make things particularly difficult for families in which the patient is resistant to accepting help, especially from someone new or unfamiliar.

- When an able-bodied person suddenly becomes disabled because of an accident or illness, they almost invariably have a very difficult time making the adjustment. Part of this adjustment involves accepting help; going through the difficult (and sometimes laborious) process of finding a good caregiver;

and building a trusting relationship with them. Many of these people need more—perhaps much more—than 40 hours of care and assistance each week. The Companionship Exemption empowers these recently disabled people and simplifies their situation. Instead of having to find, test, and work with multiple caregivers—or else pay through the nose for overtime—they only need to find one. (Or, if they need round-the-clock care, perhaps two.)

- About 1% of all home care is paid for by Medicaid—but in a country of over 300,000,000 people, that means Medicaid foots the bill for home care for hundreds of thousands of people. Under the proposed rule change, the states' cost of home care for Medicaid recipients would grow substantially.

- Meanwhile, caregivers themselves will be forced to scramble. Many who currently work twelve-hour shifts will have their hours cut back to 40 per week. As a result, their earnings will drop by as much as a third. Many will need to take a second job in another field. In an ironic and unintended twist, some will sign up with two different home care companies in order to work the number of hours they want to.

- The proposed rule change would not apply to anyone who arranged for a home care provider on their own. If you know (or find) someone who could provide assistance for your mom, they can work 50, 70, or even 90 hours a week without your having to pay them time-and-a half. The rule change would apply *only* to credentialed, screened, and verified caregivers provided through licensed and regulated home health companies. The change would thus encourage families to not work with these companies, and to try to find good caregivers on their own. But the very purpose of licensed and regulated home care firms is to make it possible for people to bring in qualified caregivers without having to do their own searching, interviewing, and screening. If you live in New York and your aging dad lives in San Francisco, it's next to impossible to find someone to provide this care for him without going through a home care company.

• Thus, the results of the proposed rule change will likely be that people will get less care; home care workers will make less money and work fewer hours; and states will need to spend much more money on Medicaid. The only people who will be largely unaffected will be the well-heeled, who will simply write bigger checks.

People listened respectfully to what I had to say. But the star of the meeting was Jim Langevin. Sitting in his wheelchair, Jim took the Department of Labor to task by going straight to the financial numbers. "There's no money to pay for this," he said. "Many home health companies are paid by Medicaid. Right now, Medicaid can barely pay for straight time. Now you're saying that it has to pay for time and a half. But we're not funding Medicaid to pay for time and a half. Neither are the individual states, which will have to pay a portion of this much higher cost."*

Jim wasn't the only leader aware of this problem. In August of 2014, the Medicaid directors of *all 50* states met with President Obama to talk to him about that very dilemma, and the difficulties that this rule change would create.

But in response to our Congressional hearing, and the meeting with the 50 Medicaid directors, President Obama and the Department of Justice didn't budge.

In early 2014, a group of home care industry trade associations filed suit against the United States Department of Labor, in the District of

---

* All the quotations in this book, with the exception of Judge Richard Leon's later in this chapter, have been compressed and paraphrased for readability. Leon's is verbatim.

Columbia federal district court, to block the rule change. The case was known as *Home Care Association of America vs. Weil.*

In August of 2014, Jim Langevin asked me, "JB, there's a Democratic fundraiser coming up in a few weeks. President Obama will be speaking at it, and he'll take questions afterward. I want you to come, and I want you to question him about the Companionship Exemption. I want him to have to explain himself to a group of his own supporters."

As anyone who knows politics or business will tell you, sometimes you have to open your wallet to get a place at the table. This was a $10,000-a-plate Democratic fundraiser. I'm a registered Republican—though, as I hope you've seen, I'm not a partisan ideologue. Jim agreed that our trade association PAC could attend for $5000.

Some Democrats doubtless gloated over this. I was fine with their gloating. I had far bigger fish to fry. I was concerned about the millions of American whose care could be threatened; the many businesses and home care workers who would likely suffer; and the budgets of all 50 states, which would be stressed or busted.

In the fall of 2014, I went to a palatial private home in Newport, Rhode Island for the event. About 50 people were there, including Nancy Pelosi and Steve Israel, who was then Chairman of the Democratic National Committee. I was probably the only registered Republican—or, at the very least, the only Jewish Republican—in attendance.

As is usual for such fundraisers, we all got in line, and each of us shook President Obama's hand and had our picture taken with him. But in the moments before my photo op, I whispered in his ear, "Mr. President, I want to give you a heads up. When you do your Q&A, I'm going to ask you about the Companionship Exemption." He said, "Thank you very much," and we smiled and shook hands and had our picture taken.

After dinner, the president gave a 15-minute talk and then took questions. I raised my hand and he pointed to me. I said, "Mr. President, on January 1, 2015, the Companionship Exemption will disappear. Caregivers in private homes who work more than 40 hours a week will have to be paid time-and-a-half for overtime. Only the wealthy can afford that. I'm an executive of a home health care agency. I'm also a person with a lifelong disability who has home care assistants of his own. And I need to tell you that I think the rule change is a mistake. Long-term care insurance won't pay for time and a half. Medicaid doesn't have the money to pay for time and a half, either. Mr. President, would you consider postponing the implementation of the rule for another 18 months so a task force can be put together to look at what changes in the law will actually be most effective?"

His answer wasn't about how to make the law work better or where the money for time-and-a-half would come from. He said, "JB, this is about equal pay for equal work. Caregivers in your home are entitled to the same pay rules as caregivers in a hospital."

I had asked a pragmatic question, but the president gave me a purely ideological answer.

To me, it wasn't really an answer. It's fine to say that people are entitled to more money. But just taking an ideological stand won't make the money magically appear.

I left the event feeling disappointed in my president.

My biggest hope now was with the District Court.

Unlike President Obama, Judge Richard Leon did not disappoint me. In two separate legal opinions—one on December 22, 2014, the other on January 14, 2015—Judge Leon blocked the implementation of the proposed rule change.

Actually, he did a lot more than just block it. He gave the Department of Labor a legal tongue-lashing. The rule change, Judge Leon wrote, "essentially would eviscerate a Congressionally-mandated exemption via a method Congress never envisioned." He also wrote that the Department of Labor's efforts to change the rule "can only be characterized as a wholesale arrogation of Congress's authority in this area!*... [T]he Department of Labor tried to do administratively what others had failed to achieve in either the Judiciary or Congress." In Judge Leon's legal opinion, he also explicitly noted that the Supreme Court had already rejected a challenge to the Companionship Exemption. Essentially, Judge Leon said to the Department of Labor, "Back off. This is none of your damn business."

So, for a short time, the Companionship Exemption remained law—good law.

But not for long. The Department of Labor responded to Judge Leon's decision by filing an appeal with the U.S. Court of Appeals for the District of Columbia.

In late August of 2015, Circuit Judge Sri Srinavasan reversed Judge Leon's decision. His rationale had to do with authority, jurisdiction, and interpretation. Judge Srinavasan noted that the dispute was not actually over the Companionship Exemption itself, but the Department of Labor's interpretation of it. And, he insisted, the DOL has the legal authority to interpret the law as it sees fit.

The changes to the Companionship Exemption took effect in October of 2015, and began to be fully enforced by the Department of Labor on January 1, 2016. In the end, I won my battle, but we lost the war.

But even the end of a war doesn't always mean final resolution. In terms of the Companionship Exemption, Congress can still override the

---

*Yes, that exclamation mark was his.

courts at any time. It can, for example, pass a new, more specific law that reinstates the Department of Labor's former interpretation of the Companionship Exemption—and makes that interpretation permanent.

Efforts to craft such a law have already begun. As I write these words, in November 2016, a national election has just been held. Many of the newly elected senators and House members have expressed their support for reinstating the Companionship Exemption. By the time this book is published, the Companionship Exemption may once again be standard policy—and federal law.

Whatever happens, I plan to stay at the table throughout the process—listening, talking, debating, challenging, and bringing the right people together in the right ways to make the wisest decisions.

~§§~ OTHER KEY LESSONS ~§§~

- Listen first—but then educate the people who don't understand.
- Don't try to rewrite rules that have been repeatedly examined and found to be wise.
- Never choose ideology over reality. You'll only create chaos.
- When you need to take concerted action, talk to lots of people.
- Don't assume that some causes are inherently liberal or conservative. Look at each case and cause on its own merits.
- Don't assume that some *people* are unwaveringly liberal or conservative. Give them the chance to look at each case and cause on its own merits, too.
- When you have to spend money to get to the table, do so if you can afford it.
- Go to court when you have to.
- If necessary (and if you can get access), go before Congress.

16

Use Your Place at the Table to Help Others—But Carefully Choose Whom You Help and How You Help Them

When I was a social worker for Home Health Corporation of America, part of my job was to visit people in their homes and interview them about their health, needs, and emotional well-being. Then I'd go back to my office, report my findings, and arrange for them to get the services and assistance they needed.

My client Angela and I got along well. She was in her seventies and a bit frail, but her mind was sharp and her manner was friendly.

Usually, anyway. But not on this Tuesday in December. When her son Tony let me in, I could see immediately that something wasn't right. Angela was half-sitting, half-lying in an armchair with her eyes closed and her arm across her forehead.

Before I could even ask my first question, she said, "JB, I can't deal with your questions today; my head really hurts. Go see your next client."

Tony nodded. "Yeah," he said, "her head's been hurting for the last few hours. The physical therapist was here for his regular appointment, but he wasn't able to help."

Something about the whole scene felt very wrong to me. I'd never seen Angela like this before. And why wasn't the PT able to do anything for her?

Angela said, "I'll call you when I feel better and we'll set up a new time for you to visit."

A light went on in my head. Suddenly I knew what was happening.

"This visit is over," I said firmly. "Angela, you're going to the hospital *right now*. You're having a stroke. Tony, call an ambulance."

"What?!" Tony said. He grabbed the phone and dialed 911.

I stayed with them until the ambulance arrived eight minutes later. When the EMTs came into the apartment, I explained the situation—and my strong suspicion that Angela was having a stroke. They took her out on a stretcher and hustled her to the hospital.

I called to check on Angela a few hours later. She had indeed had a stroke. Fortunately, the EMTs had gotten her to the hospital before it had caused any serious damage.

Somehow both the nurse and the PT had missed the warning signs.

When Angela had asked me to leave, I could have turned and left, as she had requested. Or I could have said, "Tell you what, Angela—I'll be quick today," and asked my usual questions.

Fortunately, I did neither. Because I had been alert—and because I'd been properly trained—I was able to set aside my standard duties and, instead, do what needed to be done.

When I was a graduate student in New York City, I was instrumental in helping to grow a volunteer program on the Upper West Side of Manhattan. It was called Adopt a Grandparent, and it provided companionship and social activities for seniors. Young people, mostly in the twenties, would take them to cultural events, assist them with everyday activities, and simply visit with them in their homes. A lot of these elderly folks had no friends or relatives left, so these visits were very important to them.

But the program didn't just benefit the elderly. It also provided temporary surrogate grandparents for young people. You might be surprised by how many men and women in their twenties feel an emotional hole in their lives because their grandparents live far away—or have passed on.

Many of the best volunteers were observant Jews who would leave work early every Friday and visit their adoptive grandmother or grandfather. But I quickly learned that the program needed to select its volunteers carefully.

Here's the thing about volunteers. Any volunteer is only as good as their level of commitment. Some people volunteer because they currently don't have anything better to do. There's nothing wrong with this. But the nothing-better-to-do volunteer usually disappears when they find something better—a love interest, an engaging hobby, or a new TV show to binge-watch. I can't tell you how many young people bailed out of the program once they started seriously dating someone.

I watched many volunteers come and go, and many others come and stay. Eventually I created a personality profile for the best and most helpful volunteer. Ideally, this person:

- **Is young** (so they'll have lots of energy and relatively few commitments, especially to family)
- **Enjoys some career and financial success** (so they won't regularly be rushing off to a second job, or an audition, or band practice)
- **Believes in the cause**—in this case, the cause of assisting the elderly (so the time spent volunteering will be meaningful to them)

- **Gets emotional nourishment from volunteering** that they couldn't easily get elsewhere (in this case because they had no living grandparents)

These were the people who turned out to be the most committed and reliable. They were also the people who gave us administrators the biggest return on our investment of time and support.

Over the years, I've discovered that these traits create the most committed and effective volunteers in *any* organization, no matter what its focus.

〰 OTHER KEY LESSONS 〰

- Pay attention. If you're not present and alert, you could miss something important—perhaps something life-saving.
- When something looks or feels wrong, you're almost never imagining it. Investigate.
- No matter what your standard operating procedure is, be willing to drop it when that's what the situation requires.
- Don't assume that professionals always know what they're doing—or never make mistakes.
- When necessary, take charge.
- Determine an ideal personality profile for any job, task, or volunteer position you want to fill. Then match each candidate against that profile.
- The most committed volunteers (and the most committed people in general) have plenty of energy, enough money, and relatively few other commitments. They also get meaning and emotional benefit from the role they fulfill.

---

17 To Get to the Table, Stay There, and Do the Most Good While You're There, Recruit Both an Advocate *and* a Protector

While you need at least one talented advocate by your side, you also need at least one talented caring, savvy protector. The advocate pushes you, encourages you, and helps you to succeed. The protector loves you to pieces, and watches your back to make sure you don't get taken down.

If we're lucky, when we're young we have at least one person—a parent, a grandparent, a coach, or a teacher—who fulfills one of these roles for us. If we're *very* lucky, we have people who fulfill both. I was one of the most fortunate ones. My father was my ideal advocate, and my mother was an almost-perfect protector. Together, they made a wonderful team.

You remember the story about my father and me driving to Ottawa to visit Prime Minister Trudeau. It's easy to see what a great advocate my father was for me. But my mom was also the ideal protector. When her husband said to her, "Joseph and I are taking a drive to Ottawa," she said, "Enjoy yourselves." She knew something was up, but she didn't press us for details. She trusted us to do the right thing, and she knew we'd return and report back soon enough.

When we got back almost six hours later, the table was set for dinner. My mother kissed us both and said, "Sit down and eat." She served us soup, steak, and French fries. She waited until we were comfortable and relaxed. Only then did she ask, "So, did the two of you have a good time?"

Every one of us is born an advocate. As children, we learn to advocate for ourselves more and more with each passing year. We convince our parents to let us have seconds of pie. We push them hard to get us an Xbox or a bicycle for our birthday. We use all the charm we can muster to get the cute girl or boy in math class to go out with us.

If there's something we want or like or love, most of us don't need any training to advocate for it. We naturally work to get it.

By the time we grow up, most of us have developed and honed our skills at advocating for ourselves. In adolescence or early adulthood, we also learn to advocate for others. And when we become parents, we quickly learn how important it is to advocate for our children. This is especially true for a child who is disabled.

Unlike advocates within a family, professional advocates usually need to be sought out, groomed, and/or trained. In many cases, they also need to be paid—and paid well. Yet a good professional advocate is worth every penny.

An advocate is willing to put themselves out for you, stand by you, and move and shake things for you. If you need something, they will get it for you—or find someone else who will.

But they are not your flunky or lackey. They will tell you what they think and feel and believe. They'll debate with you and point out the things you're not seeing. If they think you're about to make a bad decision, or make an ass out of yourself, they'll tell you. And they won't abandon you if you do screw up.

They won't expect you to be *their* lackey, either. They won't demand that you do what they say, and they won't get pissed off if you overrule their advice.

Your protector is an entirely different kind of person. When you stumble, they'll catch you. When they sense danger, they'll guide you away from it. And when you're exhausted at the end of a long day, they'll bring you a cup of tea, and perhaps drive you home. They'll keep you safe, and sometimes provide a bit of comfort as well.

Imagine that you're walking down the street with your protector and your advocate beside you. Suddenly an angry dog comes charging out of an alley. Your advocate will grab a stick and try to drive the dog away. Your protector will push you to the ground and lie on top of you. (I'm being metaphorical here, of course. If a dog actually attacked us, I'd lean on one cane and wield the other like a club. Or I'd hold the arm of one of the people and say, "Grab the other cane and start swinging.")

While many of your advocates and protectors need to be encouraged—and, often, paid for—this isn't always the case. Sometimes someone you hadn't expected will turn out to be one of your strongest advocates, or one of your most loyal protectors.

When I was president of the Private Care Association of America, a national trade association representing credentialed nurse registries and caregivers, my vice president, Amy Natt, turned out to be an incomparable protector. She watched out for me 24/7. When controversial items came up for a vote, she made a point of voting with me 100% of the time. When I expressed a valid but coarse opinion behind closed doors, she made sure the coarseness got removed before my critique went public. She defended me professionally to the ends of the Earth. As a bonus, she also called me out personally when I did something foolish in my personal life.

I didn't ask for this level of support, and certainly didn't expect it at first. But I was very grateful for it. Today she's the trade association's president. I hope that she has a supporter of her own who works half as hard for her as she did for me.

If you're middle aged or older, you may remember a parallel from the 1980s. When George Herbert Walker Bush was Vice President of the United States, he provided the same level and type of support to then-President Ronald Reagan. Bush had Reagan's back 100% of the time, fiercely supporting everything Reagan said and did. And, like Amy, Bush later rose to the level of president, and proved effective in that role.

It's rare for the same person to be both your advocate *and* your protector. Usually, the two roles fall to separate people, because they require very different skill sets. Advocates are often chief operating officers and program directors. Protectors are often chiefs of staff and top-level administrative assistants.

A highly talented and versatile vice president can sometimes fulfill both roles at once. But there's a big problem with such a person: because they're so capable, they're likely to soon take a job as president or CEO somewhere else.

❧ OTHER KEY LESSONS ❧

- Almost anyone can be an advocate. With few exceptions, all of us have been advocating for ourselves—and others— since we were young.
- As adults, most of us have to find, groom, and/or train our own advocates and protectors.

- Don't try to find the perfect person to fulfill both roles. It's far easier to find one person to fill each role.
- In an emergency, canes can be surprisingly useful.

18

Invite Others to the Table and Help Them Get There— Even If Some People at the Table Disapprove

Of all the lessons in this book, this is one of the most important. For me it's also one of the most painful and humbling. Not too long ago, out of fear, I violated it big time—and have paid a huge (but appropriate) price.

I'm a somewhat observant Jew. I'm not a zealot. I don't dress like I live in 19th century Poland, or refuse to sit next to a woman on an airplane, or keep my kids away from secular society. I often eat kosher food, but don't always. I dress in normal clothes, talk like a typical American, and encourage my kids to engage with the world. I observe the Sabbath—in my own way. I drive to the synagogue. Why should a guy with cerebral palsy have to walk in the rain?

I take other Jewish holidays very seriously; I like to study Torah; and I educate my kids at Jewish schools. I believe in serving the Jewish community. For two years I was president of Boca Raton Synagogue, and I'm now serving my sixth year on the Board of Overseers for the men's undergraduate college at Yeshiva University.

I'm also an adult. This means that I practice Judaism in the way I choose—not by habit or coercion.

For many years, I belonged to an Orthodox Jewish community by choice. I followed its rules and norms and expectations by choice. And occasionally, by choice, I would break one of those rules or norms or expectations. But I never did so capriciously or thoughtlessly. (Today I'm less observant, but still very consciously Jewish.)

In 2014 I got divorced, and my ex-wife and I were each awarded half-time custody of our four kids. The people in my synagogue weren't thrilled about the divorce. But what really bothered some of the people in my congregation was the woman I was dating. My girlfriend Meg wasn't an Orthodox Jew. In fact, she wasn't Jewish at all.

Not that she didn't appreciate Judaism. She was very interested in converting. She was an avid student of Judaism, and she came to synagogue with me.

The two of us also were very interested in each other. She joined me at a long string of home care industry events.

Some of the people in my synagogue disapproved of my divorce. Even more disapproved of my dating Meg—a non-Jew.

It also seemed to bother some people that Meg was pretty and sexy, drove a red Jeep, and had a tattoo. While she didn't dress provocatively, she didn't dress as modestly as Orthodox women generally do.

To Meg's credit, she wasn't bothered by what my fellow synagogue members thought of her. She had nothing against them—after all, she was interested in becoming one of them some day—but she didn't want or need their approval. She wanted *me*. "Don't worry about them and what they think," she said to me. "Just be you. And just be with me."

But the people in my synagogue were not happy with me being me, Meg being Meg, and the two of us being together.

That bothered me—a lot. I was raised an Orthodox Jew. As I've said, I don't robotically follow every Orthodox practice or custom. I strongly support the right of each person to make their own religious and spiritual choices. Still, for all of my life, Orthodox Jews had made up my spiritual community and my extended family.

I didn't want to have to choose between the woman I cared for and the community to which I belonged.

But sometimes making a painful and difficult choice is unavoidable.

Passover is arguably the third most important Jewish holiday—just after Yom Kippur, the Day of Atonement, and Rosh Hashanah, the Jewish new year. It's a time when Jews and the people we care about come together over a long dinner, called a *seder*, to retell stories from ancient Jewish history, and to reflect on the themes of exclusion, bondage, resistance, and freedom.

For Passover of 2015, which began in early April, I planned an elaborate seder in my home. In attendance would be my kids, some of my good friends, and a handful of other people from my synagogue. I wanted to remind all of them that—despite my divorce, and my relationship with Meg—I was still very much part of their tribe.

Which was fine. But then I did something foolish and misguided. I didn't invite Meg.

"When is your seder?" she asked me in mid-February. "Do you want my help with it?"

"You want to come to my seder? Why? A bunch of people who disapprove of you will be there."

"Of course I want to be there! I'm your girlfriend. Why wouldn't I want to be with you and your kids for an important holiday?"

I found myself fumbling for an answer. "Meg, I'm worried. What if some of the people there treat you disrespectfully?"

"We'll both tell them to stop. If they don't, you'll throw them out."

She was right and I was wrong. Dead wrong.

I'd spent my whole life saying to people, "Don't shoo me away or make me go off into a corner somewhere! I belong, damn it!" Now, suddenly, I found myself facing people who were telling me, "JB, you *did* belong, and we accepted you. But now that you're dating this *goy*, we're not so sure you belong at our table anymore. Of course, we're not pushing you away. You're pushing *yourself* away."

That was the message I was getting. And it hurt.

It was also a lie. I wasn't trying to separate myself from anyone. I was simply planning a holiday celebration with people I cared about. I was creating a guest list for *my* seder, in *my* home.

I should have said to Meg, "You're completely right. Join us, please."

And I should have said to my seder guests, and the members of my synagogue, "I'm dating Meg. If you don't like it, fine, that's your right. But don't give me any crap about it. She's the woman I've chosen to be with, so she'll be part of our Passover celebration."

But that's not what I said. Instead, I said to Meg, "They're my community! I can't criticize them to their faces, right at the seder table!"

But of course I could have. And I should have been willing to.

I would be at the head of the seder table—an actual table that I would set up in my own home. And I had just told the woman I cared for that she wasn't welcome at it.

I was letting other people dictate which guests I invited to my own table.

Meg sighed and said, "All right, then. Have your seder without me. In fact, have the rest of your life without me. We're done, JB."

If you're like most people, including me, when you finally get a place at the table after years of struggle, you'll have accumulated some emotional baggage. The biggest piece of baggage—your steamer trunk—will be a gnawing fear of losing that hard-won place. This fear may be understandable, but it isn't valid.

Fear of loss is never a good reason to be unfair or unwise. Never.

In fact, those of us who have been excluded have a responsibility not to exclude anyone from any table where they genuinely belong. When there is opposition or disapproval from others at the table, that is all the more reason to extend the invitation.

At the end of every seder, Jews around the world open the door and welcome in the spirit of Elijah, the wandering prophet. We also say, earlier in the seder, "All who are hungry, come and eat; all who are needy, come and celebrate Passover."

At both points in my seder that April, I thought of Meg, and of how I had let my fears shut her out of a celebration that focused on freedom. I saw how small-minded I had been.

Once we make it to the table, part of our job is to invite other people who belong there.

Sometimes some of our tablemates may say to us, "Wait a second! Who said you could invite that person?" That's when we need to take a deep breath, acknowledge our fear, open the door, and say, "Welcome."

When someone truly belongs at your table, always set a place for them—no matter what others in attendance think or say.

❧ OTHER KEY LESSONS ❧

- Follow the rules whenever they make sense. Consider breaking them when they don't.

- When you do break a rule, understand that there will be consequences.
- When faced with the choice of being yourself or getting approval, be yourself.
- Sometimes making a difficult and painful choice is unavoidable.
- When people act badly, tell them to stop. If they don't stop, throw them out.
- When people tell you that you're the problem, stop and ask yourself, *Am I really?*
- Fear of loss is never a reason to be unfair or unwise.
- Those of us who have been excluded have a responsibility to invite others to tables where they genuinely belong.

19

When New People Join the Table, Welcome Them, Even If They're Not People You Wanted Or Planned to Work With

Right after I graduated high school, I went to an Israeli yeshiva for my freshman year of college. A yeshiva is an academy for studying the Torah—the first five books of the Old Testament. The students are usually young men, ages 18 to 22. It was a challenging but instructive experience, and I was mostly glad to be there.

After two months, I visited my cousin at a different Israeli yeshiva, known as BMT, which was short for Beit Midrash l'Torah.

BMT was a very different place from where I'd spent the previous two months. The accommodations were second to none—almost luxurious. But what really made this yeshiva special was that its students weren't just young men in their teens and early twenties. Some were married men in their late twenties who received scholarships to study there after finishing their bachelor's or master's degrees. They became our tutors, our advocates, and our go-to guys.

Of course they knew much more about Torah than we did. But they also knew how to learn. So if I got stuck with something in the middle of the afternoon, they could help me out; I didn't have to wait to ask the rabbi the next day. This was an opportunity that my own yeshiva had lacked.

After spending only one day at the study table at my cousin's yeshiva, I knew it was a table I wanted to sit at some day. So I made myself a promise to return and study Torah there eventually.

Now fast forward to December of 2000. My father David had just died unexpectedly, and I was in mourning. For the next year—partly to help process my grief—I studied Torah twice a week with a rabbi from the Boca Raton Synagogue named Avi Schneider. It was the best and most fulfilling learning I'd done in a long time. Rabbi Schneider was a master teacher.

Then Rabbi Schneider left Boca and resettled in Israel, as many Jews do. Over time, I lost track of him.

But I never forgot my promise to myself. So in December of 2014, at age 46, I flew back to Israel and spent a week at the yeshiva I had visited and loved close to 30 years earlier. For that week, from 9 a.m. to 1 p.m., I sat at the same table as several dozen young men, studying Torah in English and Aramaic together.

That in itself was wonderful. But for me there was an added bonus: our teacher was Rabbi Avi Schneider.

At first I was very aware of how different I was. There were 150 students in the room, and I was old enough to be every other student's father.

But in other ways I wasn't different at all. Of the five students at my study table, two of us were disabled—and, clearly, no one saw this as an issue. I marveled at how far we had come.

As for Avi Schneider, he acted as if only a few weeks had passed since I had studied with him 14 years earlier. He even set aside an hour a day to work with me one-to-one.

BMT and Avi Schneider sent me the same consistent message: *Welcome, JB. You have a place here.* And, after 14 years, Avi Schneider deepened that message to *Welcome back, JB. You* always *have a place here.* That is one the most empowering messages that one human being can give to another.

❧ OTHER KEY LESSONS ❧

- Don't assume that two things with the same title and purpose are similar. Sometimes they can vary greatly.
- Outsiders can often offer wisdom and guidance that insiders can't.
- A great teacher can make the difference between a useful experience and a transformative one.
- When you make an important promise to yourself, keep it.
- No one is ever too old to learn.

20

No Matter How Crowded Or Noisy the Table Gets, Don't Try to Force People Out. Instead, Find Ways to Make the Table Bigger

As soon as my wife and I got engaged, we started talking about having kids. We both wanted them eventually, and I often reassured her that, yes, it would happen someday.

But we knew it wouldn't be easy, because of two interrelated problems.

First, she had a tumor on her pituitary gland, which was being held in check by a drug called Sandostatin. Her doctor told her that the drug could cause birth defects, so having children was out of the question unless she went off it. But going off it might also allow the tumor to grow, potentially risking her health.

Second, the tumor had disrupted her menstrual cycle, so she wasn't properly dropping eggs. And without eggs, you can't get pregnant.

We consulted with multiple doctors—including specialists at Harvard and NYU—but the message was always the same: *If you want kids, adopt some.*

I vividly remember telling my wife, "It's going to happen. You're going to get pregnant and have kids. I don't know how, but we're going to go forward. We're going to find a way."

Soon after we got married in June of 1995, we moved to Lansing, Michigan so that I could go to law school. There we learned about an endocrine specialist named Dr. Ariel Barkan. We were told that he had helped many couples who had had trouble getting pregnant. Dr. Barkan worked at the University of Michigan research hospital, a couple of hours away in Ann Arbor. We decided to make an appointment to see him.

As soon as we met Dr. Barkan, I could see that, like me, he was a Jew of Sephardic descent. I hoped that this was a good omen.

We explained our situation to him. Then Lisa said, "We want to have kids, but I don't know how I'm going to get pregnant."

Dr. Barkan raised his eyebrows and said, "What do you mean, how are you going to get pregnant? The two of you will have sex." Then he said, in Hebrew, "*Pru u'rvu,*" which is from the Torah, and means "increase and multiply."

This was our first ray of hope. But we were also confused. Lisa said, "But the doctors at NYU and Harvard told us that my getting pregnant would be very dangerous. The phrase they used was *high risk.*"

Dr. Barkan held up his hand. "Listen. Lots of people you see walking down the street with happy, healthy kids—they had high-risk pregnancies. If you want to have children, you can have children. Go for it."

So Dr. Barkan gave us hope—and permission.

But, though we tried our best, for the next two years pregnancy eluded us.

Not long after we met with Dr. Barkan, we moved to Boca Raton, Florida. Our neighborhood was mostly observant Jews—who usually have a *lot* of children. All around us, everyone our age was having babies. At Friday night dinner tables, our friends and neighbors talked endlessly about pregnancy, childbirth, and child raising. Lisa and I were happy for them, but she also became increasingly sad about our own situation. She felt like the odd person out, like there was something missing from our lives. At times it felt like we couldn't be full-fledged members of the Orthodox community until we had a child. Meanwhile, we kept trying, but nothing happened.

Then, one Shabbat, we met another couple that had had trouble getting pregnant, but who were expecting a child. They told Lisa, "You've got to meet our doctor, Steven Ory. He gets it right every time. If you're not conceiving, he's your guy."

So we made an appointment with Dr. Ory. His viewpoint was the same as Dr. Barkan's. He said to us, "Of course you can have kids. But to make that happen, you'll need to do more than just have sex. I'm going to give you a plan. Follow it completely and it will work."

Lisa and I looked at each other. "Okay," we both said.

Dr. Ory's plan involved a combination of sex and *in vitro* fertilization. For readers not familiar with the process, it worked like this:

First, my wife was shot up regularly with very large doses of hormones. These made her body generate lots of eggs. (It also generated enormous mood swings.) These eggs were harvested and kept alive in a lab.

Meanwhile, I was instructed to donate sperm, which were kept alive in the same lab. My sperm were let loose into the eggs, which were then reimplanted in my wife.

None of this was a lot of fun for either of us.

Not that we weren't allowed to have sex. In fact, we were told *exactly* when we could and couldn't—and should and shouldn't—have sex, according to a strict hormonal schedule that the MD understood but we did not. We would get instructions on our voice mail that said things like, "I want the two of you to have sex tonight between 8 and 11 p.m." His tone was exactly the same as if he had told us, "Your prescription is ready to be picked up at the pharmacy."

But I'm not complaining. It turned out that Dr. Ory knew exactly what he was doing. After only a month of having sex on command, plus the implantation of Lisa's lab-fertilized eggs we achieved a successful pregnancy.

And in October of 1998, our son Maurice was born—perfectly formed and very healthy.

A few years later, Lisa and I decided we wanted a second child. Once again, it didn't take long for Lisa to become pregnant. We were delighted, and began making plans to add a fourth member of our family.

Then, about five weeks into the pregnancy, we got a call from our OB-GYN, Dr. Konsker. Lisa had recently gone in for a blood test, and her hormone levels were off the charts. She was asked to come in for further tests. "Is there a problem?" we asked. "Well," the doctor told us, "there's definitely more than one child in there. Possibly as many as four."

We did the tests—and discovered that we would soon be the proud parents of triplets.

The news was wonderful—and frightening. Bringing three children to term is much harder on a human body than growing and giving birth to one. And my wife did not have a normal, healthy body. She still had a tumor on her pituitary gland. Yes, it was being kept under control through drug therapy—but the drug had its own side effects.

Dr. Konsker told us, "If you choose to carry all three babies, it's risky. The pregnancy could injure or even kill you."

I looked at my wife. Tears were running down her cheeks. She asked, "What do we do?"

Dr. Konsker said, "It's not my business to tell you what to do. But if they were my babies, I'd abort one to give the other two—and you—a better chance at a healthy life."

That option felt wrong to both of us.

Next we consulted with the senior rabbi at Boca Raton synagogue. As my wife sat crying beside him, he told us that Jewish law condoned sacrificing one fetus to spare the others—and her. Then he said, "Talk about this. Pray about it. I can tell you what Jewish law and tradition say, but I can't make the decision for you."

In the days that followed, my wife and I held each other and talked over the situation. We also prayed. And prayed some more.

Finally I said to Lisa, "You know what? God is great. He can make sure that you give birth to three strong, healthy babies if he wants to. It's no skin off his back. Let's go for it."

She was all for it, too. We also agreed that we simply weren't willing to prevent one of our babies from joining the world. Instead, we would take a risk.

Eight months later, my wife gave birth to three healthy children—two girls and a boy.

Today, although we are now divorced, my wife and I remain the very proud parents of four wonderful, smart, healthy, loving kids.

Now it's over fifteen years later. In spite of all the risks, of the six of us, I'm still the only one with any kind of disability.

⊰⊱ OTHER KEY LESSONS ⊰⊱

- When three experts agree, a fourth may nevertheless have a different view. And sometimes that fourth view will turn out to be right.

- Listen carefully to experts, and take what they say seriously. Then make your own best decision.
- The word *risky* means that something bad *could* happen—not that something bad *will* happen.
- Most disabilities are not hereditary.

21 If You Have the Opportunity and the Skills, Bring Everyone at the Table Together Into a Team

Whenever I give a talk, presentation, or workshop, I always arrive very early. This gives me time to reconfigure the room. No matter how it's set up when I first get there, I rearrange it so that everyone—from the time they sit down—feels like they're part of a single team.

Once the presentation begins, my job is not just to inform, inspire, and guide people. It's also to bring them together into a unified group—more than just a roomful of individuals.

In short, my job is to serve, not merely perform.

The same is true when I'm trying to create a specific result. Often there are many different players and many different moving parts. It's foolish to think that these will all align on their own.

First there is preparation. I work hard to make sure that the right people get put in the right places and establish the right working relationships. Then and only then, it becomes possible to orchestrate events and exert influence.

In real life, of course, things will rarely go exactly according to plan. So it's also important to be flexible and think on your feet.

Here's a prime example of the importance of bringing everyone at the table together into a team:

It's sad but true that many health insurance companies sometimes deny valid claims. This was the case some years ago with National States Insurance—which is now defunct—and one of my company's clients. National States simply refused to pay them. (Eventually I discovered that National States played this game with lots of companies. In fact, many home health care firms wouldn't even take on clients who had insurance with National States, because the company was so unwilling to pay legitimate claims.)

I understood immediately that, in order to get my own client's claims paid, I would need to align multiple players, one at a time, and create a team that would put the maximum possible leverage on National States.

First I brought the Florida Office of Insurance Regulation on board.

Then I met with Bill Nelson, who was then the state's insurance commissioner. (Today Bill is a U.S. senator.)

In each meeting, I explained the situation—and the relevant laws—in sufficient detail. Then I said, "National States is breaking the law. We need a unified voice to force them to follow it. Here's who else is already on board. Will you join us?"

Once this team was assembled, we contacted National States as a group and said, in unison, "All of us are in agreement. You need to pay this claim or face prosecution. Your choice."

At first this didn't work. National States held its ground, even with the threat of possible prosecution.

But we were an aligned team. We kept pushing back, and pushing back, and pushing back.

Meanwhile, as part of this process, I kept talking to folks at National States. I'd ask, "What *exactly* do you need us to do in order to pay our claims? And what *exactly* is wrong with the claims we've been filing?"

Under all the combined pressure, National States finally told me, "We only pay for assistance with the activities of daily living."

"I see," I said. "That's exactly what my home health care professionals have been doing."

"No, they haven't," I was told.

It was like trying to solve a riddle. I kept asking more and more detailed questions, while the rest of our team kept the pressure on National States.

"If my caregiver helps someone do the laundry, does that count as an activity of everyday living?"

"No. We won't pay for that."

"How about helping them shower?"

"Yes. We'll cover that."

"What about taking them shopping?"

"No."

"Driving them to the doctor?"

"Uh uh."

"Helping them with house cleaning?"

"No way."

"Helping them go to the bathroom?"

"Yes."

"Helping them cook supper?

"Nope."

"Helping them walk to the kitchen?"

"Yes."

Finally, with enough questioning—and enough pressure—we got National States to admit that *assisting with activities of everyday living* meant physically touching someone—helping them stand, walk, or otherwise move their body.

It also meant that unless each such form of bodily assistance was clearly and specifically mentioned in each caregiver's activity notes—and unless we provided copies of those notes to National States—it would simply refuse to pay.

With my team backing me up, I started resubmitting claims to National States. But I instructed my caregivers to write different things in the care activity notes that they had provided to me before. Instead of writing *Helped client cook dinner*, I had them write *Helped client stand, walk, and maintain balance*—some of which took place while the client was cooking dinner.

Finally we had National States cornered, and they knew it. We had sussed out the dodge they were using to refuse to pay claims.

Under the combined pressure from three directions—the state insurance commission, the Office of Insurance Regulation, and me—and with the use of the exact terminology and protocols that National States required (but had tried not to reveal), the company caved.

From then on, they paid every claim. And we didn't have to go to court over it.

Of course, I didn't stop there. Through our home care trade association, I spread the word about National States and how to get them to pay legitimate claims. Other home care companies started doing what we did, and our industry's problems with National States ended.

❈ OTHER KEY LESSONS ❈

- Before you present, reconfigure the room in the way that best serves your audience.

- It's not always enough to be right. Sometimes it's also necessary to assemble a team of people who *know* you're right.
- When you need to exert leverage, apply it from every possible direction at once, so that your target has nowhere to go except where you want them to.
- Ask questions. If necessary, *keep* asking questions until you get adequate answers.

22

Don't Let Fear Drive You From the Table. Accept the Fear, But Don't Flee.

Sometimes there are good reasons to leave a table—but fear is never one of them. I learned this the hard way.

After 15 years of marriage, my wife and I began to grow further and further apart. Both of us remained good parents to our kids, but we were not always good to each other.

One cause of our growing distance was our different views of the world. Lisa was an excellent businesswoman—and she took a very businesslike approach to life. Except for our kids, relationships weren't always a high priority for her.

One aspect of this is that she rarely accompanied me to funerals, weddings, trade association meetings, political dinners, or other events, unless she saw some clear potential benefit. She often said to me, "I get it, JB—one of us needs to attend. But you'll be there, so why do I need to show up, too? It's just a waste of my time. I could be doing something productive." This made some sense to me for trade association meetings, but much less for weddings and funerals.

In 2011, I was honored at Yeshiva University's annual Hanukkah celebration, where I was recognized in its Points of Light ceremony. This was one of the high points of my life. Naturally I wanted Lisa to be there with me, and I told her as much. But she elected to stay home. That was her right, but I felt hurt by her choice.

It was about this time that it became clear to me that our marriage had withered away—and couldn't be revived. In retrospect, it was probably clear to her, too.

But marriage isn't like a business. You don't just say, "Okay, it didn't work. Let's close up shop." The prospect of staying in the marriage frightened me, but the prospect of ending it frightened me even more. I was afraid to say to her, "This isn't working. I want to split up." I was even more afraid to say to my kids, who were then in elementary and middle school, "We're not a nuclear family anymore."

There's nothing wrong with being afraid. But there's something very wrong with letting fear guide your decision making. As adults, we need to feel and accept the fear, and then make the wisest decision we can.

What I needed to do was stay at the table, speak up honestly and straightforwardly to my wife and kids, and work out a plan for leaving the table that would provide respect and caring for everyone. This would have made all of us hurt like hell. But it also would have created a solid and honorable foundation for making the break and moving forward with our lives.

Unfortunately, that's not what I did with my marriage. I followed my fear instead of my integrity. Like many people do when they're in marriages that aren't working, I had an affair.

People think affairs are mostly about sex, but that's actually pretty rare. Usually an affair is a way to temporarily avoid living in a painful situation—and to avoid saying difficult things that need to be said. It's a way to flee.

In my case, I also loved (and will always love) the woman I had the affair with. Still, by having an affair, I created a situation that ended the marriage and split up the family, but didn't require me to tell anyone what I really felt or wanted. This wasn't fair to anyone. (I didn't realize any of this at the time. It took me three years—and sessions with a psychotherapist—to understand the underlying dynamics.)

And, in case you're wondering, I'm no longer involved with the woman I had the affair with. I lost her, based on some serious mistakes I made. Which is yet another reason to think twice before having an affair. If you're foolish enough to have an affair rather than speak the truth to people, you're not likely to act wisely in the relationship you're having on the side.

I've provided the example of my marriage, but similar things can occur in all kinds of contexts: at work, with relatives or neighbors, and with making decisions of all kinds. We feel trapped at the table where we're seated, and we know we need to leave—but we're scared to speak up and tell the truth. Maybe we're afraid to accept the truth about our situation. Maybe we're afraid to change—or face an unknown future. Maybe we're afraid to hurt other people. Maybe we're afraid of all of the above. But fear is no reason to act irresponsibly.

The truth is that having an affair is stupid. It only causes pain and problems for everyone. If your own marriage has crumbled and you want to take up with someone else, fine—but do it honestly, respectfully, and in the proper sequence. End the marriage honorably first before leaping into someone else's arms.

I wish I had been wiser about the end of my own marriage. But when fear bit me in the butt again later on, I had learned enough to respond differently.

When my affair became public, which almost always happens, some of my friends told me—emphatically and in detail—that I had been a total schmuck. This didn't surprise me too much, and I sat still for their tongue lashings. But they weren't the people I was worried about.

Remember, I'm an Orthodox Jew, a former president of my synagogue, a member of the Board of Oversees of Yeshiva University's undergraduate men's college, and a part of other important boards. I'm tightly tied into the Orthodox Jewish community. I was afraid of what that community would say and do when it learned about my affair— with a non-Jew. I worried that I would be asked to resign from some of the boards—especially at Yeshiva University and the Orthodox Union.

Part of me said, *They're going to tar and feather you. Resign from everything before they kick you off.*

But by then I had learned something about fear. Instead of acting from it, I swallowed hard, took some deep breaths, and went to some key people for their advice.

First I asked another member of Yeshiva's Board of Overseers, who had the ear of the president of the university, if he felt I should resign. His response was thoughtful, honorable, and practical. He told me, "No, JB. Please stay. Naturally, nobody here approves of what you did. But we need you and your perspective on the board. Your affair didn't diminish your value to us and to Yeshiva."

Next I swallowed harder and met privately with the executive vice president of the Orthodox Union. I half expected him to tell me what I foolish, selfish jerk—and what a bad husband, father, and Jew—I had been. But he did nothing of the sort. Like the fellow from Yeshiva, he told me that he disapproved of what I'd done—though he also added that I was hardly the first board member to have done something less than 100% ethical. Also like my colleague at Yeshiva, he asked me to stay on.

If only I'd been as honest and straightforward with my wife and kids as I'd been with these two gentlemen.

Now I'm divorced, and my ex-wife and I live mostly separate lives. But I am very grateful that neither I nor Lisa walked away from the parenting table.

Now I live in St. Petersburg, Florida, less than four hours from my kids by car. I'm planning my second run for the Florida House of Representatives, and working as the Vice President of Evergreen Private Care. All four of the kids—who are now in high school—are doing great. The divorce was not as hard on them as I'd expected, and they continue to love and respect both their parents.

﹡ OTHER KEY LESSONS ﹡

- There's nothing wrong with being afraid. But there's something very wrong with letting fear guide your decision making.
- When you're afraid, feel and accept the fear, then make the wisest decision you can.
- If you feel trapped at the table where you're seated, and you know you need to leave, speak up and tell your tablemates.
- Having an affair is stupid. It only causes pain and problems for everyone.
- If your own marriage has crumbled, end the marriage honorably before leaping into someone else's arms.

---

23 When Fear Threatens to Drive Others From the Table, Help Them to Stay

In the mid-1990s, before my wife and I moved to Florida, I worked as a substitute middle school teacher in Lansing, a mid-size city in the heart of Michigan (and the state capital).

Lansing is a tough town. In many of its schools—even middle schools—you have to pass through a metal detector to get inside. Even with those protections, on occasion kids somehow manage to bring guns to class.

Many of the kids needed far more than just academic instruction. From my first day of work as a sub, I saw my role as a combination of teacher, advocate, and protector.

As I worked with the kids in my classes, I often remembered Glenna Chinks, my sixth-grade teacher at Hebrew Academy in Montreal. She had been a tireless advocate for me throughout that school year. Now she became my role model for working with the kids in my own classroom.

For the most part, my kids were typical adolescents going through the normal tribulations of puberty. A few, though, were routinely disruptive. I dealt with each disruption as best I could, on a case-by-case basis. One thing I never did was shame any student for their behavior. How could I? I had been the single most disruptive child in my own elementary school's history.

On one occasion, I even told a student who was acting out, "Listen, I know you think I was born in a coat and tie at the age of 25. But when I was younger than you, I got pissed off and threw a desk out my classroom window."

His eyes went wide. "No b.s.. You did that?"

"No b.s.," I said. "I did."

Still, one morning two young men caught me completely by surprise.

Class was about to begin, and most of my students had taken their seats. As I waited for the bell to ring so we could get started, two young men suddenly stood up, looked each other in the eye, and pointed handguns at each other.

The class went silent. Time stopped. The scene felt like the climax of an old western—except that both gunslingers wore baggy jeans, and neither one could have been more than 14 years old.

In a split second, two scenarios played out in my mind. In the first, I imagined one of the young men firing his gun in fear and panic. Then the other boy fell in a bloodstained heap, and an ambulance arrived and took him to the hospital. In my second mental scenario, I imagined a terrified principal banishing both kids from school—and putting an education forever out of their reach.

In social work training, they don't teach you what to do when two adolescents point guns at each other. But they do teach quite a lot about defusing a crisis. And I understood intuitively that my job was to keep both boys alive, safe, and in school.

If I didn't have cerebral palsy, I would have immediately stood up. But for me, *stand up* and *immediately* don't go together. I would have needed four or five seconds, and I didn't have that kind of time.

So, from my seat, I said—loudly, calmly, and firmly—"Gentlemen! Put your guns down."

They did.

"Good," I said, just as firmly. "Thank you. Now, please sit down."

They took their seats. The boy closest to me was shaking.

"Excellent." I looked at a girl in the front row. "Felice, go to the office and bring back the security guard." She nodded and hurried out of the room.

I said to the class, "We're going to spend the next minute or two just sitting quietly. Stay in your seats." To the two young men I said, "The security guard's job is not to arrest you or hurt you. His job is to keep each of you safe. I don't want either of you leaving this room with a bullet wound. When he gets here, he'll give you instructions. I want you to follow them carefully. He'll disarm both of you in a way that keeps you and everyone else out of danger. Nod or say yes to let me know that you understand."

One of the boys nodded; the other said, "Yeah. I got it."

Soon the security guard arrived and temporarily took charge. It was clear that he had been trained in a step-by-step protocol for just such a situation—and that this was not the first time he'd had to follow it. Soon both young men had been disarmed.

By the end of the period, my classroom was more or less back to normal.

When I got home that afternoon, my wife asked me, "How was your day? Did anything interesting happen?"

I set down my canes and sat on the couch. "Yes," I said. "I may have saved someone's life."

About two years later, when I worked as a social worker for a Medicare-certified home health agency in Boca Raton, part of my job was to visit people in their homes, assess their situations, and determine what resources they needed.

That was my intention when I made my first visit to my new client Martin's home. Martin was in his 80s. He lived with his wife in a nondescript middle-class neighborhood. A home care worker came by each day for a few hours to assist the couple.

I knocked on Martin's door, and after half a minute it opened. Bonnie, the home care worker, stood in front of me, with a very concerned look on her face.

"Good morning," I said. "I'm JB. Can I come in?"

Bonnie didn't answer. She turned sideways so I could see inside the apartment.

Martin stood behind her in the hallway. His arms were outstretched toward us. In his hands, pointed at us, was a pistol.

"Come in," he said softly.

Even in Lansing, I'd never been welcomed in and threatened with a handgun at the same time.

I was frightened, of course. But something told me that I needed to engage with Martin and his wife—and that if I stayed calm and present, everything would work out okay.

I stepped inside.

Martin's wife Ida was sitting at their kitchen table. With his gun, Martin motioned for Bonnie and me to sit on either side of her.

As calmly as I could, I said to Martin, "Tell me what's going on."

Martin sighed. "I'm going to tell you the whole story. I need you to listen, okay?"

"Okay," I said.

"Ida keeps telling me that I have depression and that I belong in the hospital."

I looked at his wife. She looked back at me with great sadness—and a bit of terror—in her eyes. "Yes. I've been telling him that for the past three weeks." To her husband, she said, "Martin, put the gun down. JB's just a social worker. He's not a policeman."

Martin didn't move. "Ida's wrong about the depression," he said. "She needs to stop badgering me about it." The barrel of his gun was pointed straight at my face.

I nodded. I said, "Maybe she's wrong and you *don't* belong in hospital. I haven't been here long enough to be able to tell. But one thing I know for sure is that you don't really want to shoot anybody. If you shoot your wife—or Bonnie, or me—and one of us dies, you'll be in jail the rest of your life. That's a lot worse than being in a hospital."

To my surprise, Martin set the gun on the kitchen counter, next to the toaster.

When he turned back to me, his eyes were filled with sadness. "I need you to listen to the whole story."

"Of course," I said. "I'm listening."

For the next half hour, Martin and I had a conversation. He talked about his disappointment with his life, how nothing had gone the way he had wanted or planned. He told us about dreams that had unraveled, hopes that had been dashed, and efforts that had gotten thwarted. I said little and mostly just let Martin speak. Occasionally I asked him to elaborate. A few times, I simply said, "Go on. I'm listening."

As a social worker, I learn a great deal about many people's lives—and I had long ago discovered that every human life has many disappointments and tragedies. Still, Martin's life did sound like it had been tougher than most.

When he was done talking, I didn't threaten him or tell him that he needed help. Instead, I let him know that he was important, that he belonged in the world and in his marriage, and that both were worth staying in.

When I was done, he looked at me and said, "You want some coffee?" That's when I knew we were out of the woods.

As the four of us sipped coffee, I said to Martin, "Here's what I suggest. I can have the police drive you to the hospital—not to be committed, but just for an evaluation. And you won't be arrested. I don't bust people. Neither will the police, when I explain the situation.

"Once you're there, the police will drive away. At the hospital, mental health professionals will evaluate you and suggest a course of action or treatment. I don't know what they'll say, but at least you'll get a professional opinion. Can we do that?"

Martin looked at each of us, one by one. He took a sip of coffee. "What the hell. Sure."

I dialed the police and explained the situation. The dispatcher said, "A patrol car should be there in ten minutes."

In Florida, police routinely make hospital trips, so the situation was very familiar to them. When the patrolmen arrived, they were friendly and cooperative. Nobody in the room wanted my client arrested, so no arrest was made and no charges were filed.

Martin went to the hospital content, fully accepting that he needed to be evaluated.

It turned out that Martin and Ida were both right. At the hospital, doctors evaluated him and decided that he *did* have moderate depression—but that he didn't need extensive hospitalization. They told him he'd probably improve with medication and counseling. They asked him to stay in the hospital for three days as a precaution, and he agreed. When those three days were up, he was given a counseling appointment and a prescription, and sent back home.

I stayed in touch with Martin for several months afterward. The counseling and meds turned out to be all he needed. Although he was still disappointed with aspects of his life, he was able to stay in his marriage and in society.

∼ OTHER KEY LESSONS ∼

- No matter what your job title and job description are, you may often need to go beyond those boundaries in order to help another human being in need.
- Regardless of what is happening, do your best to stay calm and present.
- Don't try to be a hero. When you need backup, call for it.
- Two of the most useful and important words in the English language are *don't panic.*

24

When Others Already at the Table Need Your Help, Offer It—But Don't Force It On Them

Most people think that someone is either consistently able-bodied or permanently disabled. But of course that's not true. Temporary disabilities, created by injuries or illness, are far more common than permanent ones. In fact, if you're 20 years old, there's a one in four chance that you'll become disabled before you retire. Most likely, this disability will be temporary.

Even many permanent disabilities are only disabilities in certain situations. For example, I can do anything an able-bodied person can except ride an escalator. (This is because of my two canes and the way I walk.) So, strangely, I can climb stairs just fine, but I can't use an assistive stair-climbing device.

When people offer me a wheelchair or a supporting hand on my arm, I smile, shake my head, and say, "Thanks, but I'm good."

Interestingly, it's usually the folks who are temporarily disabled who need the most help. If you think about it, this makes sense. A 40-year-old woman who has been in a wheelchair most of her life may be able to do figure eights with it, pull wheelies in it, bowl in it, and play basketball in it. Meanwhile, her brother, who is healing from a hip fracture and who has been in his own wheelchair only a week, still has trouble getting it over parking-lot speed bumps.

When we celebrated my son Maurice's bar mitzvah, one of the guests—a 13-year-old classmate—showed up on crutches. He'd always walked fine before, so we asked him what had happened. He told us he had recently broken his leg. He was clearly new to crutches and was having trouble getting around.

Maurice noticed this. Soon after the bar mitzvah ceremony was over and the reception began, he stopped what he was doing, went up to his seated friend, and said, "I'm headed to the buffet to get something to eat. Want me to fill a plate for you?"

His classmate looked relieved. "Yeah, cool. That would be great. No celery, okay?"

I managed to eavesdrop on this interaction, and I was proud of my son for several reasons. First, he was thoughtful enough to notice his classmate's situation, and to realize that he might appreciate some help. Second, he was kind enough to offer that help. Third, he was wise enough to emphasize that it was no big deal. He wasn't making some special effort or trying to perform some charitable deed. He was just casually making himself available. Fourth, even at the age of 13, he understood the importance of letting his friend say yes or no.

Maurice knew, in part from watching his dad, that not everyone with a disability wants help all the time. Maybe his classmate would *want* to practice navigating a buffet line on crutches. So he said "Want me to fill a plate?" rather than "I'll fill a plate for you."

A bar mitzvah is a rite of passage in which, in terms of Jewish ritual and religious status, a boy becomes a man. I spent the next few minutes thinking about how apt the day's ceremony had been, because Maurice had done a very adult thing.

But then, over the next few minutes, something even more interesting happened. One by one, each of my other three children—each one eleven years old—went up to the boy with his leg in a cast and, on their own initiative, made the same offer.

I asked them about this later. They each told me that what they did was simple, obvious, and automatic. They saw the buffet, saw the boy with crutches, and said to themselves, *If I don't do something, he might not get to eat.*

I was proud of all four of my children that day.

~❀~ OTHER KEY LESSONS ~❀~

- When someone looks like they *might* need help, don't assume that they do or that they don't. Ask them.
- When offering your help, make it easy for someone to say yes—*and* easy for them to say no.

25

When Other People Who Belong at the Table Won't Come to It, Insist That They Do

For years, I was president of the Private Care Association, a national trade association. The PCA advocates for companies that provide in-home care for the elderly and disabled.

But not for every company. Only for our members.

When someone from a member organization would call me, I would always help them as much as I could. This often involved making calls and sending e-mails to powerful people on members' behalf. It meant lobbying to change bad laws—and keep good ones. Sometimes it meant offering guidance and advice to company executives.

Strangely, leaders of some home care companies didn't really understand what a trade association is. They thought of it as a community resource or public utility. When they'd call me up and ask for my help, I'd say, "Hang on. Your company isn't a member."

"No," they'd say. "But—"

"Well, if you want my help, become a member. You know how to go online, click and paste, and pay dues. Call me back once those dues are paid." And, most of the time, they *would* join, pay dues, and call back. Then I'd say, "Welcome. How can I help?"

For several years I was also the president of the Boca Raton Synagogue, where I followed the same principle. Religious services and fellowship were always free, of course. But if you wanted something more—religious school for your kids, counseling from the rabbi, participation in a class or synagogue group—then I'd say to you, "Become a member. If you're coming to the synagogue every week and using our lights and air conditioning and rest room, we don't want you be an outsider. Become a formal part of this community. We'd love to have you. But if you're not paying dues just because you'd prefer not to, I've got no time for you." I was never mean or dismissive about this— just very clear.

None of this was about the amount of money; it was about commitment. Standard dues for a family were $1800 a year, but if you couldn't afford that amount, I'd say to you, "Pay what you can. If all you can afford is $100 a year, that's fine. Commit to that amount and you're welcome to everything our synagogue has to offer."

In some cases, people *were* poor. We set their dues at $100, and once they paid those dues, we accepted them as full members with open arms.

And you know what? Everybody got it. At both the synagogue and the trade association, people intuitively understood that I was being fair. Not once did someone push back, or grumble, or tell me I was asking too much. And most of the time, people joined.

To me, this was about justice. You shouldn't expect to reap the benefits of membership without sharing in its responsibilities.

Imagine that you walk into Costco. When the greeter says, "Good morning; may I see your membership card?," would you say, "I'm not a member, but I want some bargains. Can I come in anyway?" And if you did, would you really expect the greeter to let you in? Or would you expect them to laugh and point you to the membership desk?

~∰~ OTHER KEY LESSONS ~∰~

- Don't ask for things you're not entitled to.
- If you want something, do what is required to *become* entitled to it.
- Be clear about any commitment that people need to make to sit at a particular table. Then hold them to it.
- When you set fair and reasonable terms for joining a table, people will understand. They will also respect you for it.

26

When Someone at the Table Tells People That They Don't Belong, Challenge and Educate Them

For 16 years I was CEO of an organization called United Elder Care Services. Our main business line was a nurse registry. When people in south Florida needed someone to care for a sick or elderly relative, or if they were sick or elderly themselves, they called us. In 2004, my wife and I also opened a Medicare-certified home health agency.

When I sold United Elder Care in 2014, we had served over 8,000 clients and had over 400 caregivers in our registry. We had a great reputation with our consumers, and as a business we were very successful. We felt we had a caregiving model that worked for everyone. In short, we were comfortably seated at the home health care industry table.

Then, in 2011, a family that wanted to use United Elder Care's nurse registry services called us to complain—but not about us. The family *wanted* to do business with us. But they told my administrator that their insurance company wouldn't pay for care provided by our nurse registry. The insurer had banned this registry from its own particular corner of the health care table.

That made no sense to me, so I investigated.

The insurer was a huge company in Chicago called CNA. It turned out that our potential customers had a long-term care policy with CNA, and the company would only pay for home health care if it was provided by a Medicare-certified home health agency.

As I said, my wife and I operated such an agency, as well as a nurse registry. But this particular customer wanted to use the registry. This was a matter of practicality, not principle. The family wanted to use a particular caregiver whom they liked and trusted, and who had been certified, verified, and screened by our nurse registry. But she (of course) wasn't an employee of the Medicare-certified home health agency, and CNA refused to pay for that caregiver because our nurse registry was not Medicare certified.

This may sound reasonable enough at first. But in practice, it amounts to an insurance company telling you that it will refuse any package sent to it via Federal Express. If you don't ship it using UPS, they'll send it back to you unopened.

Sounds crazy, right?

This all had to do with two different models for offering services to customers. Each one has its benefits and its drawbacks. Think cable vs. satellite TV, or UPS vs. Fed Ex.

One model is the independent contractor or registry model, which Fed Ex follows. The person who delivers your Fed Ex package has their own delivery business, which contracts with Fed Ex. Because they're an independent contractor, they typically make more money per hour than their UPS counterpart.

The other model is the employee or agency model, which UPS uses. The person who delivers your UPS package is an employee of UPS; they receive a regular salary, plus (in many cases) employee benefits. Those benefits have value, so they largely balance out the lower hourly earnings.

It's clear that both models work. Both Fed Ex and UPS provide very good service, and both companies are extremely successful.

The home health care industry operates according to these same two models. At some organizations—the ones that follow the agency model—caregivers are on the company payroll. Other companies follow the registry model, in which independent caregivers contract with the home health care organization to deliver services, just as Fed Ex drivers contract with Federal Express to deliver packages.

Caregivers who are independent contractors typically make considerably more money per hour, but receive no benefits. As I write this chapter in early 2017, a typical home health care company in Palm Beach County, Florida might charge clients about $18/hour for the services of a home health aide or certified nursing assistant. Under the employee or agency model, the aide or CNA might earn about $9/hour, plus (perhaps) benefits. Under the independent contractor or registry model, they might earn about $11-12/hour, but receive no benefits.

Companies that follow the registry model often charge less than those whose caregivers are employees, because their costs are lower. This obviously benefits consumers.

A bit paradoxically, though, the registry model also allows a customer to pay an exemplary caregiver more—at the customer's sole discretion, of course. For example, if Beatrice has been providing wonderful care for your aging father, you can call the registry and say, "Bea has been great. I'd like to reward her by raising her hourly rate." The agency, which normally takes a simple percentage of whatever the consumer pays, will say, "Great! Pay Beatrice whatever higher rate you want. We'll take our percentage and pass on the rest to her." You can't do this for a salaried employee who works for a home care organization using the agency model.

Some people take sides. They pit one model against the other and say that one is great and the other stinks. But to me that's absurd. Clearly, both models work. In fact, as I said, my wife and I owned an employee-based home care agency *and* a nurse registry that followed the independent contractor model.

I believe in and strongly endorse the registry or independent contractor model. In fact, I'm the former Executive Director, and former President, of the Private Care Association, a national association that advocates for consumer choice in private home health care, as well as for the rights of the independent caregivers who serve those consumers. But the employee or agency model also creates good results for customers. (Ask yourself this question: *Does UPS suck, while Fed Ex shines—or vice versa?*)

Which brings us back to Medicare and the insurance company CNA. Medicare regulates and certifies most home health care organizations that follow the employee or agency model. But companies that follow the independent contractor model are typically licensed and regulated by individual states. Medicare doesn't, can't, and won't regulate or certify them. There is literally no such thing as a Medicare-certified nurse registry, just as there is no such thing as an AARP-approved preschool or a USDA-approved smartphone.

In part this is simply because of how our health care system evolved. But it's also because a nurse registry often offers forms of home care that Medicare doesn't pay for, such as help with cooking and household chores.

All of which is fine—until an insurance company says, "If it's not regulated and approved by Medicare, we won't pay a penny for it."

That's exactly what happened with CNA. It said to our potential customers, "If you're going to arrange for care from a nurse registry, you aren't welcome at our financial table. The people who provide care through any nurse registry aren't welcome, either."

This was clearly unfair. If a potential client chooses another company because they like it better or it does a superior job, that's fine. But refusing to do business with a huge swath of legitimate companies isn't in anyone's best interests.

My wife and I decided that we needed to prove two points: first, that the distinction CNA had made was arbitrary and absurd; and, second, that in refusing to pay for services provided through a nurse registry, the insurance company was breaking the law.

I called my potential customers back and explained what I knew. Then I told her, "What CNA is saying is unfair and illegal. I know you want to work with our nurse registry, and we want to work with you. So I'll make you this deal. You hire us, just as you would if CNA were paying for it. We'll pay all our independent contractors at our own expense. We won't ask for a penny from you. We'll run a tab for the cost and bill CNA. I know they're going to refuse to pay—but we're going to take them to court. If we win, they'll have to pay the whole tab. If we lose, all your father's care will be free."

At first the daughter, who was a lawyer, thought I was crazy. United Elder Care was a local company worth a few million dollars; CNA had assets of over fifty billion. To her, this wasn't David vs. Goliath; it was David vs. a nuclear bomb.

But I had made her an offer that was hard to refuse. "If you put it in writing," she told me, "it's a deal."

I wanted her and her father as customers, of course. But not just them. CNA had probably told hundreds of other south Florida families that it wouldn't pay for any services provided by the nurse registry run by United

Elder Care. God only knew how many other insurance companies were telling thousands of other potential customers the same thing.

But this wasn't just about United Elder Care not having access to thousands of potential customers. All of our competitors that used the registry model were also being excluded. They deserved the chance to compete for these customers, too.

So United Elder Care began providing care for the father. We billed CNA, which of course refused to pay, month after month.

Meanwhile, I looked more closely into the law. It turned out that in Florida, state law is very clear: home health companies that follow a registry or independent contractor model, and those that follow an employee or agency model, must be treated equally. You can't discriminate, just as you wouldn't be allowed to discriminate against Fed Ex or its drivers.

So, in 2011, United Elder Care filed suit in Florida State Court against financial giant CNA.

As I and my lawyer prepared our case, I called a bunch of my competitors and asked them about CNA. They all told me the same thing: "CNA won't pay us, so we don't provide services to any of their policyholders." I thought, *What a waste.*

At the time I was 41 years old, and a relatively seasoned businessman. Yet I felt exactly the same way I had when I was in elementary school. I thought, *This isn't right. I need to challenge it— and I'm going to win.* I never felt, even for a moment, that I had the slightest chance of losing. I knew in my heart and gut that we'd get paid every penny from CNA.

That helped me keep going as the months passed and the unpaid tab grew—to $50,000, $75,000, and eventually to over $100,000. Meanwhile, we kept paying the caregivers.

As the court date approached, CNA made it clear that it had no interest in settling or otherwise coming to terms outside the courtroom.

They seemed to feel they were in the right just as strongly as I felt that I was. But not for the reasons you might expect.

The issue I and my lawyer were arguing had to do with consumer choice. Why shouldn't a policyholder have the right to choose whatever home care provider they want, so long as its charges are reasonable and it's properly licensed and regulated? Furthermore, what difference does it make whether it's regulated by the state government or Medicare? To us it was a question of fairness for both home health care companies *and* their customers.

Yet, in the back and forth between lawyers that took place as the trial date grew closer, CNA didn't even try to argue that point. They said, in essence, "We acknowledge that Florida has a statute that prohibits discrimination. But our position is that we don't have to comply with it."

According to CNA, the issue was that our customer had bought the long-term care policy years ago in Pennsylvania—and Pennsylvania had no statute explicitly prohibiting discrimination against home health agencies that followed the registry model.

So, CNA argued, it was perfectly legal for them to discriminate under Pennsylvania law. Yet they were planning to argue this in *Florida* state court.

My lawyer and I were stunned. The argument wasn't just weak; it was *stupid*. Was CNA suggesting that I could (metaphorically) discriminate against a Fed Ex driver whenever a package they delivered had been mailed in Pennsylvania?

Countering that argument would be ludicrously easy. "So," I had my lawyer ask his CNA counterpart, "are you saying that if somebody buys a life insurance policy in Chicago and they die in Florida, the insurance company doesn't have to pay a death claim because the person died in a different state? Or that the death isn't official until it's certified by an Illinois coroner—so the family has to ship the body to Chicago?

What about the premiums that United Elder Care's customer paid on the long-term care policy? Those were mailed from a different state. Do they not count?" CNA's lawyers, as well as the people they reported to, were deeply unmoved.

Around this time, I met with Kevin Rader, a member of the Florida House of Representatives (and a Democrat), and explained the CNA case to him. He shook his head and said, "I know someone who's a lobbyist for CNA. I'm going to call him and tell him that CNA needs to stand down and pay the claim. I'm also going to educate him about who he's up against. I'll tell him, 'You're picking a fight with JB Bensmihen. Bad idea. You're going to lose.'"

Kevin did just that, but the lobbyist told him, in essence, "No way. We're not paying that claim. Ever."

Next I called my friend Jeff Atwater, the Chief Financial Officer for the state of Florida (and a Republican). Jeff was in charge of nearly all business regulatory issues for the state. We agreed to meet for breakfast.

It was a long breakfast. For two hours I outlined the case for Jeff. When I was finished, he said simply, "JB, I'm going to take care of this."

Jeff was true to his word. Before the end of that day, Jeff called CNA and said, "Listen to me. I know the law, and you guys are violating it. I'm going to give you a choice. You can pay the claim in full, or I'm going to audit every pending case you have in the state of Florida."

The person Jeff spoke with said, "No. We're still not paying the claim."

I know this sounds hard to believe. At the time, *I* didn't believe it. My lawyer didn't believe it. Probably Jeff Atwater didn't believe it.

As it turned out, the CNA board of directors didn't believe it, either.

Like most boards, they weren't aware of many of the specifics of the company's day-to-day operations. But soon after Jeff's phone call, they got wind of what was happening. They were not happy.

The CNA attorney got fired. The lobbyist got fired. A whole string of people who had made or supported the decision to deny my customer's claim got fired.

CNA sent United Elder Care a letter that said, in essence, "Oops! Sorry. Our bad. We promise to always pay your claims from now on." CNA also sent us a check for every penny that was due, plus interest.*

Sometimes the other people at the table won't explicitly say, "You don't belong"—but they'll keep asking, "Are you *sure* you belong?" until you either go away or stand up to them. I believe in standing up.

A few years ago, my family was vacationing in Las Vegas. There's a zip line right downtown, and my son Maurice, who was 12 at the time, told me he wanted to go zip lining. I said sure. So, one night, long after sunset, we took the elevator up 45 stories to the beginning of the zip line. As soon as we got to the top, an employee looked at me and my two canes and asked, "Sir, are you sure you can do this?" I said, "Of course."

We went to the locker room to get our equipment. In the locker room, a different employee saw me and asked, "Are you certain you can do this?" I told him, "Sure."

Once we were suited up, we walked to the start of the line to get strapped in. There a third employee, a young man with a crew cut, said to me, "Are you sure you can handle this?" When you think about it, it's a completely crazy question, because when you're on a zip line your feet don't touch the ground. A zip line is just about the *only* place where I can move as fast and as smoothly as anyone else—and one of the few places where I don't need a cane. So I said, "I'm fine. Let's do this."

---

* I hope I've made it clear that CNA not only ultimately did the right thing, but its key leaders evidently would have supported doing the right thing from the start. The bad decisions and bad behavior came from a small group of CNA employees, not from a policy decision made by its top people.

That's when my son turned to the young man and asked, "Why do you people keep asking my dad that question? He can do anything that anyone else can do."

The guy with the crew cut smiled and gave us a thumb's up, and off we went.

⚛ OTHER KEY LESSONS ⚛

- When you know you're right, don't worry about the size, wealth, or power of your opponent. Sometimes just being right is enough.
- When you *really* want to get or keep a customer, make them an offer that's simply too good to refuse.
- If you have friends in high places, ask for their help.
- If your job is to protect your employer's interests, don't do it by acting stupid and stubborn.
- When people ask you whether you belong at the table, say yes. If they keep asking, keep saying yes until they hear it.

27

When Someone at the Table Tells You That *You* Don't Belong, Get Everyone's Attention—and Then Educate Them

L obbyists are paid to educate legislators. Unfortunately, in many cases they're also paid to mislead legislators—and, all too often, they succeed.

In the previous chapter, you read about the two business models in the home care industry: registries (a la Federal Express, whose delivery people are independent contractors) and agencies (a la UPS, whose delivery people are employees). In 2009, lobbyists for home care agencies convinced Representative Doug Holder of the Florida state legislature to sponsor a bill that would have given agencies an unfair advantage over registries. The lobbyists told Doug that the bill was about consumer protection. They tried to make the case that care provided by an independent contractor was inferior to care provided by an employee.

This was absurd, of course. The lobbyists were just trying to gain market share at registries' expense. But they had Doug's ear, and they were starting to convince him.

I wasn't happy about this. At the time, my company, United Elder Care Services, included both an agency and a registry, and I wanted these two business units to continue to complement each other, not compete.

So, through the registry industry's lobbyist, I scheduled a meeting of my own with Doug Holder.

Holder was no fool. He wanted to make sure that no one was feeding him b.s. So he also invited to the meeting key players from an agency trade association, the National Private Duty Association, which had also been pushing him very hard to sponsor and pass the agency-friendly, registry-unfriendly bill.

All of us met in Holder's office. He asked me to make my arguments first.

I explained to him the realities of agencies and registries, and told him exactly where to look to corroborate every detail I provided: IRS records, workers' compensation records, and so on.

Then it was the agency lobbyists' turn. They made their case, most of which was bogus nonsense. I sat and listened quietly, knowing that I had done more than just make a good argument. I had the facts on my side.

After two hours of listening, Holder sent us all away, and asked us to return to his office at 5:30.

When we reconvened, the meeting was brief and to the point. Holder barely even glanced at me. He looked the agency lobbyists hard in the eye and said, "I'm retracting my own bill. It does nothing to protect consumers. Everything Bensmihen told me—*everything*—is true." His tone grew more severe. "I want you to know something else. In the future, don't you *ever* ask me to sponsor one of your bills again."

~ OTHER KEY LESSONS ~

- It's important to be able to make a strong, sensible argument. But it's even more important to have the facts on your side.
- When you invite someone to pitch you, also invite someone to make the opposite pitch—preferably at the same place at time.
- When an industry spokesman tells you how good (or bad) something is for Jane and John Doe, the only thing you know for sure is that it is good (or bad) for that industry.
- Break someone's trust once and you may lose it forever.

28

When You Need to Solve a Problem, Call to the Table People With the Necessary Skills. Don't Just Call People With Good Intentions.

This is the fundamental principle for solving any problem. Yet in practice, it's often overlooked—especially in federal and state legislatures, where the prevailing idea is *When there's a problem, the best people to solve it are politicians.*

This is completely backward. Politicians' main job is not to have good ideas and wise solutions. It's to solicit good ideas and wise solutions from the right people, and turn the best ones into law.

I've been very closely involved with the health care industry all of my life. I've been a patient, a volunteer, a caregiver, a manager, a home care business owner, an advocate, a social worker, an adviser to federal and state legislators, a lobbyist, an organizer, and an association president. Because I lived for two decades in Canada and almost three decades in the United States, I've been able to closely compare the different health care systems. I'm in a unique position to see what can work in the U.S.—and what never will.

Let's start with something that won't work: Obamacare. It had noble goals, but it simply didn't work very well in its first couple of years of implementation. Its predecessor, the Massachusetts-based Romneycare, didn't work very well, either. Neither the Democratic Obama nor the Republican Romney recognized their programs' primary flaw: each one forced large numbers of people to pick a health care plan they didn't particularly like.

In health care, as in so many forms of human activity, if you have to force people to do something, it's because they don't want it or it doesn't work. If something *does* work, you won't have to force people to use it, because they will naturally gravitate to it.

The problem behind both Obamacare and Romneycare is that they were created primarily by politicians—people who don't fully understand the economics of health care.

The job of designing any state or national health care program should be delegated to people who design health care plans for a living: actuaries. We'll come back to these people shortly.

In order to fix the American health care system, we need to start not with something that doesn't work, but with something that does. The United States already has an excellent health care program: Medicare. Americans are very happy with Medicare. I don't believe an American has *ever* said to me, "Medicare sucks. When I turn 65, I'm not going anywhere near it. I'm buying my own private insurance instead."

So, one part of the solution is to take an already popular program—Medicare—and make it available to everyone.

If this idea makes you uncomfortable because it's socialized medicine, get over it, because Americans really, really like Medicare. If you think they're wrong to like it, then for the next month try telling everyone you know, "We need to take Medicare away from our elderly neighbors, because it's socialism." Then let me know how things work out for you.

On the other hand, if you're thinking, *Wait a minute, JB. Medicare's going broke. It's not sustainable,* you're completely right. We can't have a health care system that goes broke. So we need to fix the economics behind Medicare.

That's what our politicians probably won't do. But a group of competent actuaries can.

Making Medicare sustainable isn't rocket science. Just call to the table a nonpartisan (or bipartisan) group of experienced actuaries. Say to them, "Figure out what American workers and employers can reasonably afford. Then, based on that amount of money, figure out how much health care we can pay for. Design a bunch of different programs around those numbers, and make sure each program pays for itself. Then bring us all the options and we'll pick one."

I don't know what the actuaries will come up with. But any plan they come up with will stay solvent—and will give every American citizen reasonable health care coverage. Our current system does neither.

I'm sure that some aspects of Medicare will need to change. Maybe it will eventually kick in age 67 rather than 65. Maybe the cost of the plan will need to go down gradually between the ages of 64 and 70. Maybe some things that are currently covered will need to become optional, for an additional charge. Maybe the market for Medicare supplements will expand to cover people of all ages. This is all fine, so long as the plan is based on solid economics, not ideology.

Whatever plan gets implemented, it will surely need tweaking. That's fine, too. People will be very vocal, and very public, about what works and what doesn't. Congress can listen to them for a couple of years, then bring the actuaries back to the table and say, "Here's what people are saying. Come up with some fixes." And they will.

Some years ago, the University of Wisconsin built a group of new buildings around a large open area. Once the buildings were ready to use, they did something—or, rather, didn't do something—that I consider genius. Instead of putting in walkways, and trying to force people to walk in certain patterns, they left the area bare for an entire academic year. During that year, the university's planners paid close attention to where people actually walked.

The next summer, when they put in the walkways, they were exactly where they needed to be, because they weren't based on some planner's grand idea, but on the real people who schlepped back and forth across the open space.

❊ OTHER KEY LESSONS ❊

- Whenever possible, build solutions around what people already accept and like—not around what they dislike or resist.
- Get advice and information from people who actually know something—not just those who imagine they do.
- Don't imagine that you know exactly what other people want. Instead, ask them.
- Better still, observe their behavior.

29

Never Forget the People Who Helped You Get to the Table

Nobody becomes successful entirely on their own.

While many of us have overcome obstacles or challenges, this never happens in a vacuum. We rise through the ranks, or build a strong business, or make a profound difference *within* society, in relationship to other people.

Nearly all of us have also received important assistance or inspiration from others. Without their efforts and generosity, we wouldn't be where we are today.

Many of the stories in this book are about what *I* did to make a difference. But, as you've seen, my success also owes a great deal to what others did to make a difference for me.

In 1993, I applied to the master's program in social work at Wurzweiler School of Social Work in New York. Wurzweiler is part of my undergraduate alma mater, Yeshiva University. I was pleased to be accepted, but there was no way I could afford the cost of the program— well over $40,000 (and this was in 1993). In order to attend, I needed financial assistance, so I applied to the school for a loan.

Instead of a loan, I got a call from a stranger: Jerome Lipschitz, the director of Canadian Friends of Yeshiva University. Jerome explained that Yeshiva had told him about me, my plans to become a social worker, and my need for financial assistance. He asked if we could meet at his office in Toronto. Of course I said yes.

In the days before our meeting, I repeatedly wondered what he would want or expect from me. Would he ask for a commitment to work for him once I'd gotten my master's degree? That seemed unlikely, since he did not work in a social service field. Would he ask me to go to Israel and be a social worker there? I kept trying to figure out what his hook or catch or angle might be.

It turned out there wasn't one.

My meeting with Jerome lasted almost two hours. He was pleasantly humble and straightforward. He asked me lots of good questions, and we discussed a wide range of subjects. At the end of our meeting, he said to me, "Our goal for you is the same as yours. We want you to get a master's degree in social work so you can make a good living, get married, have kids, and do well in life. We're going to give you a full tuition scholarship for your master's program. You'll still need to cover your own living expenses, but the cost of your education will be zero."

At the end of our meeting, I thanked him, we shook hands, and he wished me well. The two of us never met again.

I often wonder where my life would have gone without this generous financial support from people who barely knew me, and who asked for nothing from me in return.

When my wife and I founded United Elder Care Services in 1998, one of our first clients was a very wealthy, powerful, well-known businessman. I'll call him Michael. His elderly mother, who had just had surgery, was about to be released from North Broward Medical Center. She had chronic health issues and needed round-the-clock home care.

I didn't know Michael at all, except by reputation. His secretary had found a list of home health care firms and called us. I called back and Michael took the call. He said, "I'm ready to do business. What will my mom's 24/7 care cost?"

Back then, the price was $4400 per month. That's a lot of money now, and it was a lot more money then. But I quoted Michael the price, he said, "Fine. I'll have my secretary send you the money in advance."

She did. But she didn't send $4400; she sent a personal check from Michael for $10,000.

I called her and explained that her boss had overpaid us. She told me, "JB, my instructions are to send you ten thousand dollars a month."

I was stunned. I simply said politely, "Okay. Thank you."

For the next seven years, we received a $10,000 check from Michael every month. There was never a note or an explanation— just $5600 extra.

During those seven years, I never met or spoke with Michael. But my wife and I were both deeply grateful to him. That extra money was crucial to getting our young enterprise off the ground. It also proved instrumental in helping us build United Elder Care into a multi-million-dollar business.

After several years, Michael's mom became seriously ill and needed to go back into the hospital. So I went to visit her.

When I walked into her room, Michael was standing next to her bed. Since he and I had never met, at first he had no idea who I was. But I recognized him from photos in *The New York Times* and *The Wall Street Journal.*

I introduced myself to Michael, and the two of us conversed with his mom until she grew tired, closed her eyes, and fell asleep.

Michael and I went out into the hall. I said to him, "Michael, I'm very grateful for your longtime trust, and for all your business. I know that you could have gone with any home care company in the area. Why did you choose us?"

He smiled and said, "Because you called me back first."

There's an important addendum to this story. Every Wednesday at Evergreen Private Care, I lead an all-staff meeting—and at every meeting I retell the end of that story. Then I add, "We were able to build a multimillion-dollar business because I called someone back first."

Everyone on my staff has the story memorized by now. Most are probably sick of hearing it. That's fine—so long as they return all their business calls ASAP.

When someone calls you, they're calling you for a purpose. *They need you.* Or, at least, they need *somebody.* If they have money to spend, you want that somebody to be you.

Don't wait. Call them back as soon as you can.

And if there are three calls you need to return and one of them is to someone you don't want to speak with, make that call first.

You'll always do the things you want to do. It's harder to do the things you don't want to. So don't procrastinate; that only extends your discomfort. Make the call and put the pain behind you.

⚞ OTHER KEY LESSONS ⚟

- Always return business calls as promptly as possible.
- Express your gratitude for other people's generosity.
- Be generous yourself.
- At times generosity comes with strings attached—but sometimes all people want is for you to succeed.

- Ask your customers what they appreciate about your products or services.

30 Always Remember That Service Is Part of the Price of Being at the Table

If what you're doing isn't a form of service—whether it's serving your country, your community, your family, other human beings, or a meaningful cause—then it's important to ask yourself why you're doing it.

I'm not saying don't do it. But you need to be clear and honest with yourself about your motives. Maybe the activity is fun or brings you pleasure. Maybe it makes you feel safer or more secure. Maybe it's an unavoidable responsibility. These are all solid motivations, so long as your actions don't harm others.

But when you're not serving others *and* you don't examine your actions and your motives, you may put other people in harm's way—and you may set yourself up for pain or failure.

Of course, it's possible to focus on service and still fail. It's never enough just to serve. We need to serve wisely, efficiently, and successfully. We've all met people who served others in a naïve, foolish, or overly expensive way, and who wound up doing more harm than good.

When it comes to service, good intentions aren't enough. It's better to take on two tasks and deliver on both of them than to take on ten and only deliver on one. Think of all the politicians who promised us the moon and actually delivered only two small craters. They disappointed us more than they served us.

What if, instead, they had promised us two or three good craters? We'd think, *I can trust this person. They delivered on their promises. I'd vote for them again.*

Behind most successful forms of service is an awareness that every big success grows out of small successes. When we look at successful government agencies, social service programs, and charities, we see this principle over and over. The key is to start small, adjust things to get them right, and then scale up.

It's also true that the more methodical and successful you are in completing small projects, the more effective you can be in handling bigger ones. As you grow a small but successful form of service into something bigger, you'll naturally develop a sense of what works, what you need to do differently, and what pitfalls to avoid. This is way more sensible than starting out big and having to make big, costly, and often embarrassing adjustments.

One other observation on service: not everyone has the same opportunities to serve. Each of us has to work with whatever opportunities are available to us.

Suppose you're a teenager who loves baseball. If your parents have money, they might spend $5000 so you can be a batboy or batgirl for a day at a Major League game. If you're fortunate enough to serve in that position, that's great. Be the best batgirl or batboy you can.

But maybe your parents don't have money, so instead you need to sell peanuts in the stands all summer to earn money for college. This is still an opportunity. Be the best peanut seller you can, serve your customers as well as you can, and congratulate yourself each time you deposit your earnings in the bank.

Of everyone I've ever met, no one was more focused on service than my mother Alegrina.

I was born nine weeks premature. I weighed exactly one pound. That's the weight of a sirloin steak for two.

From the time I was born, my mother did everything she could to help me grow, keep me healthy, and help me succeed in life. From the beginning, her efforts paid off. By the time I was three months old, I weighed five pounds, four ounces.

When I was one year old, my pediatrician advised my mother to do physical therapy with me. He instructed her to have me do five minutes of exercise, then wait for an hour, then do five minutes more, for eight hours a day.

My mother's native language is Spanish. At the time, her English wasn't very good, so she didn't understand the doctor's instructions correctly. She had me doing exercises for an hour at time, eight hours a day, with five-minute breaks in between.

That turned out to be exactly what I needed. The doctor was amazed at how much stronger my legs became.

For the next 15 years, my mother Alegrina helped me with hours of physical therapy every day. Where she most threw herself into service, though, was at Montreal Children's Hospital.

To address my cerebral palsy, I needed a series of operations on my legs. The first of these took place when I was two; the last occurred when I was 16. In all, I had 14 surgeries, though usually two would be done at the same time, one on each leg.

After each operation, I spent more than two weeks in the hospital, recovering. My mom would stay in the hospital with me—all day, every day—throughout my recovery. She even slept at the hospital on those days.

For the first few surgeries, I was so young that I didn't understand that this was unusual. I thought that having regular operations, and having your mother stay at the hospital while you recovered, was a normal part of growing up.

As I got older, though, I began to understand how unusual my situation was. And how unusual my mother was.

My mother didn't just serve me. At the hospital, she was also a beloved volunteer who cared for hundreds of other children. These children were flown in from all over Canada—Vancouver, Winnipeg, Toronto, Ottawa, the Yukon—for highly specialized care. Often they arrived without any other relatives to look after them or keep them company. My mother played with them, read to them, fed them, sat with them, and helped some of them walk.

These children were all ages, from toddlers to young adolescents; some were Christian, some Muslim, some Jewish. My mother didn't care. To her, they were just children who needed caring and attention.

None of this seemed particularly special to me. I was used to my mom serving me, so it made perfect sense to me that she would serve other kids in the hospital, too. In my young mind, serving people was what my mom did.

But it *was* special, of course—so special that, on March 8, 1974, Montreal Children's Hospital bestowed on my mother its Mother of the Year award. (March 8, of course, is International Women's Day.)

As I write this, I'm looking at a photo of my mom holding the award and smiling. Also in the picture is Farah Diba, the wife of Mohammed Reza, the Shah of Iran.

I remember my mother receiving the award, but I have no recollection of the Shah's wife. When I asked my mother about Diba, she simply said, "She was at the hospital that day, so they asked her to stand in the photo with me."

Here are some of the results of my mother's commitment to loving service: my memories of Montreal Children's Hospital are surprisingly happy ones; hundreds of other children had more pleasant and comfortable hospital stays; and my mother had an unlikely meeting with the famous wife of an even more famous world leader.

❧ OTHER KEY LESSONS ❧

- It's better to make a realistic promise and deliver on it than to promise a lot and deliver only a fraction.
- Start small; adjust things to get them right; then, once you've achieved small but consistent success, scale up.
- Not everyone gets the same opportunities in life. Yet each of us needs to make the most of whatever opportunities we have.
- It's fine for service to begin with your family and your home. But it doesn't need to end there.
- When you serve others wisely and well, people take notice.

31

Sometimes It's Much Harder to Stay at the Table Than It Is to Get to It

You'll recall that, when I was a teenager, I completed two 26-kilometer walkathons using my two canes. They weren't easy, but they weren't memorably difficult, either.

Now fast forward three decades. In late 2015 I was invited to walk in the Miami Marathon, which was to be held on Sunday, January 30, 2016. I was also asked to give a kickoff speech at a Friendship Circle banquet the night before.

As you know, Friendship Circle is a Jewish organization that serves children and young adults with special needs. Many of the people at the banquet were planning to participate in the marathon. The timing of the event was also apt, because February—the month that would begin two days later—is Jewish Disability Awareness Month.

Giving a speech would be easy. I wasn't so sure about the marathon. The last time I'd walked 26 kilometers, I was looking forward to going to college. Now I was nearing my 50th birthday. Still, I said yes to both—in part because my son Maurice encouraged me. He planned to walk and run in the race, too.

But I'm not stupid. I told Maurice, "I haven't spent the last year training for this. And I'm not a teenager anymore. I'll sign up to do a half marathon, not the whole thing."

Maurice said, "Fine."

I knew I couldn't just pop on a pair of old sneakers and start walking. So, on Saturday evening, I went to Sports Authority. I told the salesman that I needed shoes for walking a half marathon, as well as gloves for handling two canes for 13.2 miles. He said, "I've got just the shoes for you. They're pricey, but they've got special cushions, and they're extra comfortable." So I bought the shoes, plus some new gloves, and headed down to Miami, about an hour away.

That evening I gave my speech and jazzed up the crowd. The event was a grand success, and it didn't break up until about 10 p.m.

Here's what most people don't realize about the Miami Marathon: participants need to arrive at 4:30 a.m. And by the time I got home from the banquet, it was very late. I got to bed at about 1:30.

My alarm went off 90 minutes later. To my surprise, I felt energized and excited. I quickly showered and put on my running clothes. These included the jersey the Friendship Circle had given me. It displayed the Friendship Circle colors, teal and royal blue, and had a slogan endorsing me in my run for political office.

I knew better than to drive down to Miami. By the time I was done walking, my feet were going to hurt, and I had no idea how well I'd be able to use them for driving. So I called an Uber and showed up in Miami at 4:30 a.m.

I was one of 20,000 people participating in the marathon. Lots of people walked with canes, and hundreds of participants were in wheelchairs. (The people in wheelchairs started the race a little earlier than those of us on foot.)

For people at the front of the pack, the Miami Marathon is very much a race, but for a lot of people near the back it's more like a parade, so some other participants pushed strollers, or followed on roller blades or bicycles.

Here's what most people also don't realize about the Miami Marathon: January mornings in Miami can be *cold*. That morning the temperature was 44 degrees. That's perfect marathon weather after you've gone a few miles. But as you wait to start, your teeth are chattering and you're shivering like a wet dog in a blizzard.

Finally the race began. I took off.

In a minute or two I had found my stride. Although I was near the back of the pack, I moved faster than some of the able-bodied folks. I was pleased to discover that the gloves and shoes were every bit as comfortable as the sales clerk had promised me.

After 90 minutes, I was no longer cold. In fact, despite my lack of sleep, I felt good. I passed one mile marker after another. Surrounding me were people of all ages, sizes, and colors, from all parts of the world. Some of them nodded or smiled at me. They gave me strength, endurance, and support.

When I reached the nine-mile marker, there was my son Maurice, catching his breath. I took a short break, too, and we took a couple of photos together.

By now my hips, knees, and back had begun to hurt. I started to feel how different a 16-year-old body is from a 48-year-old body. But I took off trucking again.

When I reached mile marker 11, I was seeing double, and one of my feet was beginning to swell. I felt like Rocky just after being battered by Apollo Creed.

I wanted to keep going, but I reminded myself that I wasn't just walking in a marathon. I was also running for political office. And I didn't want my fellow Floridians—or my family—to pick up the newspaper on Monday morning and read *Candidate Bensmihen Collapses and Dies in Miami Marathon.*

I'd already walked for six hours and 20 minutes. It was time to stop.

The marathon has a bus that picks up people along the route. When it came by, I flagged it down and got on.

When I got back to the starting area, I took off my shoes and iced my throbbing foot. Then I called an Uber and headed home.

That evening, my kids asked me, "Dad, how do you feel about how you did in the marathon?"

I said, "I feel good."

"Then we feel good about what you did, too."

It turned out that some other also people felt good about my 11-mile walk. Here is what Rabbi Yossel Kranz, who also participated in the marathon, wrote on his blog:

13.1 miles; it's not even a full marathon. To my running mate Joseph "JB" Bensmihen, however, it might as well have been Mt. Everest. Diagnosed at birth with spastic cerebral palsy, Joseph's parents were told he would never walk.

This past Sunday, I ran the Miami Marathon and Half Marathon with Team Friendship Circle of Virginia. Of course I didn't properly train—rabbis know everything—but nothing could have prepared me for the feelings of awe and humility when I learned that our guest speaker, JB, was going to run with us…

People with disabilities are incredibly tenacious. Most of the time they refuse to allow their disability to prevent them from living their dreams. But there's something else; they also seem to have unselfish, noble, much bigger dreams.

As my hips screamed in pain (I didn't even know my hips could hurt!), all I could think was: If people who were given disabilities can turn them into blessings, what is the obligation for those who were given capabilities? If a disability can serve as the impetus for making the world a little brighter, than how much more should one's ability!

I may have finished the race faster than JB, but he was so far ahead of me [that] all I could do was hope to catch his tailwind...

❀ OTHER KEY LESSONS ❀

- Whatever you need to accomplish, make sure you have the right clothing and the right equipment.
- Know when it's time to stop.
- Then *do* stop.
- Nothing you do takes place in a vacuum. When you do something worthwhile, you never know who will be inspired by it.

32

Never Take Your Place at the Table For Granted

Life is messy, complicated, and uncertain. No one can navigate it on their own.

Success is usually messy, complicated, and uncertain, too. No one becomes a success solely from their own efforts. Other human beings help us succeed.

Each of us also needs to know that someone is watching our back. Without this knowledge—and without at least one advocate to do the watching—it's next to impossible to do great things.

This is why we all need to regularly watch out for each other and be advocates for each other. We also need to ask for help when we need it—and to provide what help we can when the situation and our abilities warrant it.

So, please, make a point of regularly thanking every advocate you have. And if you don't yet have at least one reliable advocate, do what you can to find one.

When I was a child, every night before I went to sleep, my father would tell me, "Joseph, you're the best" (or, sometimes, "Joseph, you're great"). He said this simply and straightforwardly, as if he were stating a fact that he learned at the library.

Today those words still echo in my head. For decades they have given me confidence and strength.

Now, looking back as an adult, I understand that only a narcissist would take those words literally. But I also realize that, even as a child, I never believed that I was the finest human being on the planet. Instead, I believed the essential message behind my father's words: *Joseph, you belong.*

So, if you're a parent, I offer you this advice:

If you want your own child to grow up strong and confident, tell them they're the best once a day. If you have more than one child, say those words daily—and separately—to each of them.

As your kids get older, they'll eventually ask you, "How can we all be the best? Only one of us can." Just smile and say, "You're right. It's a tie."

And when a child leaves the nest, if they haven't already figured out what *You're the best* really means, feel free to tell them: "I don't actually know who the best human being on the planet is. But here's what I know for certain: in this family and in this world, you belong."

In the deepest caverns of our hearts, those are the words each of us most needs to hear.

And the truth is that each of us *does* belong, simply because we were put here on the Earth. There is nothing more empowering or inspiring than this knowledge.

Of course, belonging is not a panacea. You also need to hold your kids accountable for their actions—and, as they grow up, to learn to hold themselves accountable. Fortunately, belonging and accountability go together.

All of us occasionally get told *You don't belong.* When we lose a job, when our application is denied, when a romance or friendship ends, or when our partner or friend or close relative is angry with us, that is the message we hear. And in that limited context—with that particular person or group, in that specific situation—we may genuinely *not* belong.

Yet if you know in your heart and belly and blood that you *do* belong here on Earth, you will be able to pick yourself up, dust yourself off, and move forward. You will also stay grateful for the knowledge that you always have a place at this planetary table.

~ OTHER KEY LESSONS ~

- Regularly thank each of your advocates.
- Ask for help when you need it.
- Help others when the situation—and your abilities—warrant it.
- Every day, tell each of your kids that they're the best.
- Every day, remind yourself that you belong on this Earth.

Part 3

LEAVING
THE TABLE

33

Think Twice About Leaving the Table When Someone Needs You at It

As you've read, when I was a child I had a long string of orthopedic surgeries to address the defects caused by my cerebral palsy.

The most difficult and painful surgery occurred when I was 16. This surgery—the final one of the long sequence—involved taking a piece of bone from my rib and inserting it into my ankle.

By then, I understood that very, very few people underwent the knife every year or so. I also understood that this would be a major operation—and that if something went wrong, it could injure or kill me.

For the first time, I was old enough and informed enough to be frightened of surgery.

With my mother, I arrived at Montreal Children's Hospital the night before my operation. We went up to my room, where I watched television for an hour or so. Then I climbed into bed and fell asleep.

I was awakened at 5 a.m. Then I was escorted into a prep room, where the hair on my chest, legs, and hip was shaved off. Next I was dunked in a bathtub of disinfectant and wrapped from shoulders to toes, like a swaddled infant. Then I was put on a gurney and left alone, to wait for the surgeon and nurses to arrive.

For over an hour I lay there, unable to move. People walked past, ignoring me. As the minutes passed and no one paid any attention to me, I grew more and more frightened. My brain understood that nothing was wrong, but my 16-year-old body and spirit wanted to break out of my bonds.

Because I'd been in this hospital for operations many times, I'd gotten to know one of the night nurses, Vicki Wright, quite well. Over the years we'd become quite friendly. To me, she had become like an older sister.

As I lay on the gurney feeling scared and alone, I wished that Vicki would magically appear, talk to me, and help me calm down. But I knew it was already well past 6 a.m., which meant that she had already gone home.

At about 7 a.m., an orderly greeted me and wheeled me down to the operating room. In appearance, he was the exact opposite of Vicki Wright. He was huge and muscular, and he had a strange haircut. He was friendly enough, but I felt like I was in a horror movie, being wheeled into a mad scientist's lab by his strange assistant.

When we reached the operating room, he left me alone once again. By now I was shaking with fear. I felt completely vulnerable and helpless.

Then a familiar voice whispered in my ear, "Hi, Joseph. I'm here." A hand lightly touched my neck—one of the few exposed parts of me.

It was Vicki Wright. She'd seen that I would be operated on in the early morning, so she stayed on—long after her shift was over—to offer me her comforting face and voice.

She saw that I was shaking, so she covered me with several blankets. She said, "The doctors are ready and everything is set up. It's all going to go fine, just like it always has."

Then she kissed me on the cheek. If I could have moved my arm, I would have reached out and squeezed her hand.

"Thanks," I said. I took a deep breath. "Okay, let's do this."

"Here we go," Vicki said. "Time to rock and roll."

The OR doors opened and she wheeled me in.

⚛ OTHER KEY LESSONS ⚛

- Keep an ear to the ground for situations where you may be needed.
- Make friends with people in places that are important to you. You might need them someday.

---

34 If You Realize You're at the Wrong Table, Find a New One

When I received my master's degree in social work, I knew I wanted to make my living by advocating for others. But at the time I also felt that an MSW degree wasn't enough. I wanted to become a lawyer—though I wasn't exactly sure what was involved in getting a law degree.

I applied to several different law schools. Most turned me down, but I got into Thomas Cooley Law School, which is affiliated with Western Michigan University in Lansing. So my wife and I moved to Lansing, and in January of 1996 I started classes.

Not everyone has the skills to be a strong advocate, and not everyone has the ability to be a successful lawyer. I already knew that I had the skills and personality to be a good advocate. But it took me only a few months of law school to discover that I simply didn't have the aptitude to practice law. I studied hard, but at the end of my first term, my highest grade was a C+.

I could see that the legal profession was not a table at which I belonged.

This had nothing to do with my legs and everything to do with my brain. I'm good at advocating for people, public speaking and presenting, making deals, supervising people, and running businesses. But I discovered that I'm not very good at citing legal precedents or understanding the nuances of legal language.

At the time, all of this was quite humbling. I was a guy who with a normal brain but abnormal legs who had overcome all kinds of obstacles. Even with my abnormal legs (and two canes), I could walk a 26k walk-a-thon. But with my 100% normal brain, I couldn't hack law school. (I later discovered that lots of people bail or flunk out of law school—and even more apply but don't get admitted.)

So, after that first term of law school, I knew I would have to look for a different way to become an advocate. So I cut my losses and began looking to other fields for a career.

This turned out to be one of the best decisions I ever made. It led to our move to Florida and the birth of our home care business, which eventually made my wife and me millionaires.

⁓ OTHER KEY LESSONS ⁓

- High aspirations and hopes are important—but so is knowing when your aspirations exceed your abilities.
- There are multiple types of intelligence. It's possible to be very intelligent in some ways and not especially intelligent in others.

- Sometimes being normal leads to failure, because sitting at certain tables requires people to perform far beyond normal.
- Cutting your losses and moving on might be your key to success in some other field, profession, or venue.

35

If Other People Force You Away From the Table, Lick Your Wounds and Find Another Table

W hen you're born disabled, you grow up with a deep yearning to contribute to the world. Because other people do so much for you, you want to take that same spirit of generosity and service out into the world.

But when I was a teenager, nobody would hire me because of my disability. I could easily have pumped gas or bagged groceries or flipped burgers or answered phones. Who needs to walk perfectly to flip burgers or answer phones? But back then, no one was remotely interested in hiring someone with cerebral palsy for a summer job. (Thankfully, things are very different today, at least in the United States—in part because of the ADA.)

Things began to improve around the time I became an adult. In 1992, soon after I graduated college, I got my first real job through a social service agency, Jewish Vocational Services of Montreal.

I was an investigator in the foreign exchange division of the Bank of Montreal. I started work at 4 a.m. and left in the early afternoon. My job involved reconciling the thousands of international banking transactions that had taken place the day before. This required some intelligence, some mathematical ability, and plenty of attention to detail. It did not require the ability to walk normally.

I loved the job. It was meaningful; it paid well; my colleagues respected me; my superiors were happy with my performance; and I got to wear a suit every day. I felt on top of the world.

I also proved my value to the bank when I noticed that some pattern in the transfers didn't look right. The more I looked at it, the fishier it seemed. I brought it to my boss, who was understandably shocked.

We looked into it in depth, and we figured out that a trusted senior bank employee had been embezzling funds for some time. My boss called in the authorities, and the employee went to jail. I was briefly something of a hero.

After I'd worked for the Bank of Montreal for six months, my boss called me into his office and told me that the bank was letting me go.

I was stunned. "Why?" I asked. "You've always been happy with my work."

"Your work has been fine," my boss told me. "But the grant paying your salary was for six months, and now it's expired."

No one had told me anything about a grant. In any case, I knew that the bank still needed to pay someone to reconcile all its international transactions. I didn't understand why that person couldn't be me, and I said so.

But the Bank of Montreal was unmoved. If it was going to pay someone out of its own funds to reconcile its international transactions, evidently it wanted someone who didn't walk funny, rather than someone who did the job well and had proven his value.

For a few weeks I felt very sorry for myself, and for disabled people in general. Then I said to myself, *We need more advocates. What can I do to make a living as an advocate? I have some work experience and a good work reference under my belt. How can I leverage them?* That's when I applied to the master's program in social work at Yeshiva University.

In retrospect, I'm grateful that the Bank of Montreal cut me loose. If it hadn't, today I'd probably be a middle manager in a financial institution in Montreal, living a few blocks from where I grew up. My life would be fairly comfortable, but it would have been far less of an adventure than the life I've actually had the good fortune to live.

⊰❀⊱ OTHER KEY LESSONS ⊰❀⊱

- Three good questions to ask yourself are:
  — What does the world need?
  — How might I earn a living by filling that need?
  — What experience, abilities, and credentials can I leverage to earn a living in that way?
- Sometimes losses—and unpleasant surprises—can be turned into opportunities.

36

Sometimes Leaving the Table Can Be a Strategic Step Toward a Place at Another, More Desirable Table

As you might recall, in 2016 I ran as a Republican for the Florida House of Representatives in Pinellas County, which includes much of St. Petersburg, Florida. But I didn't run a typical campaign. For one thing, it was clean and honest. (My Democratic opponent, Ben Diamond, ran a clean campaign as well.)

For another, I didn't fully toe the Republican Party line. I wasn't a mere mouthpiece for its platform. I ran on the Republican ticket as a proud independent voice.

Like many Republicans, I strongly support businesses and want to reduce burdensome (but not legitimate) regulations on them. Also like most Republicans, I want our tax dollars to be spent on critical community priorities, not frivolous pet projects. Like almost all

Republicans, I'm mostly a fiscal conservative. And, like every Republican I've ever met, I support the Second Amendment.

Like many Democrats, however, I believe in expanding Medicaid and improving American's access to health care. I support women's reproductive rights. I believe in keeping guns out of the hands of criminals. And I'm a firm proponent of civil liberties for everyone. I believe that if I have to put someone else down to advance my own position, then there must be something wrong with my position.

I'm proud of the position I take on each of these issues. I even printed a palm card, which I handed out to large numbers of voters, which lists some of these positions. Throughout my campaign, no one needed to guess about where I stood on anything. I didn't pander to anyone. When someone asked me why I took a particular position, I was happy to explain it to them.

As a result, a lot of people voted for me who disagreed with me on at least one important issue. These people told me, "JB, I don't like where you stand on some things. But I like *you*. You're smart, honest, and genuine, and straight-talking. You don't b.s. people. That's why I voted for you."

To their great credit, the Republican Party of Pinellas County was fine with every one of the positions I took. They were backing me as their candidate, not as a parrot who could perfectly recite the party line. They also felt that I helped to create a bigger tent for the party.

That's why, in a traditionally liberal district, I got a lot of votes from Democrats. Some people even told me that they voted an almost-straight Democratic ticket, with one exception: me. Some of these voters were lifelong Democrats who had never voted for a Republican before. As a few of them said to me, "I like Ben Diamond, but I like you more."

I did some highly unusual things in my campaign. I didn't run TV ads. Instead, I had my car wrapped, so that it was a traveling campaign brochure. Every time I drove anywhere, people saw my name, my face (at 10 times its actual size), and the office I was running for. It was such an effective promotional tool that I'm surprised at how few other candidates use it.

But the most unusual thing I did was show up in person near polling places. In Florida, people are able to vote not just on election day, but for 12 hours a day, every day, during the two weeks before an election. Each day during those two weeks—all day, every day—I stood outside a polling station in the most liberal part of my district. I introduced myself to people as they arrived to vote, handed them my palm card, urged them to ask me questions, and talked with them about whatever was on their minds.

Democrats would say to me, "You're a Republican? Forget it." Then I would say, "Listen, I'm right here. Ask me whatever questions you want. I'll listen to what you have to say and give you my honest answers. Ben Diamond, the Democratic candidate, isn't here. If you want to reach Ben Diamond, you'll have to send him an e-mail."

And people did ask me questions—lots of them. Some of them challenged me. In the end, many of them changed their votes from Ben Diamond to me.

At first, many gays and lesbian voters couldn't believe that I was both a Republican and a firm supporter of LGBTQ rights. After they voted, some of them said to me, "JB, I voted for you."

One afternoon, a devout Muslim woman, draped in cloth from head to toe, asked me, "What's your position on the right to life?"

I said, "I believe in a woman's right to choose."

She shook her head and said, "I can't vote for you."

I said, "Let's talk about this. You have only two choices on the ballot. The other is a diehard Democrat who takes the same position on abortion that I do. But let me tell you something about my own children." I told her the story you read in Chapter 15, about when Lisa and I had to decide whether to abort one of our triplets.

We prayed about it, and decided to trust in God and keep all the babies. I added, "I don't believe that you should be able to just get an abortion whenever you want, for any reason. But as a man, I'm never going to be the one getting pregnant. So I believe it has to be the woman's decision."

She didn't like my answer at all. But when she came out from the polling station, she came up to me and said, "I voted for you."

I was out in public for 168 hours, talking to people face to face, convincing them to vote for me. After we talked, some of them told me, "I like Ben Diamond, but I like you more. You're right here, and you give a damn."

I actually like Ben Diamond, too. From the beginning of the race, he and I treated each other graciously and respectfully.

As soon as he won his primary, I called him and left a voice mail message congratulating him on his win. I told him that I looked forward to us running a clean, exciting, issue-focused, fun race. He called me back the next day and we had a pleasant conversation.

The next time we talked was in early fall. The St. Petersburg Chamber of Commerce was hosting an event on the evening of October 11 called Popcorn and Politics. All the candidates for a variety of positions were invited. Anyone who wanted could show up, talk with them, and ask them about their views. The event was a cross between political speed dating and a cocktail party, but with snacks instead of alcohol.

The event was a great idea—but the timing couldn't have been worse. The evening of October 11 was the beginning of Yom Kippur, the most important Jewish holiday, and the one and only time that year in which the *Kol Nidre* prayer would be sung. For Jews, it's a major event. Many Jews who stay away from synagogue all year would show up that evening for the *Kol Nidre* service. And during Yom Kippur, Jews traditionally fast.

The Chamber of Commerce had scheduled Popcorn and Politics at the same time as Yom Kippur and *Kol Nidre*.

Like me, Ben Diamond is Jewish. So, about a week before Yom Kippur, I called him on his cell and asked, "Ben, where are you going to be on Tuesday night?"

"Tuesday night? Synagogue."

"Me, too. What about the Popcorn and Politics event?"

"I'm not going. It's Yom Kippur."

"Me neither," I said.

My campaign manager called Ben's campaign manager, and they strategized. The two of us wound up having a separate breakfast meeting, on a different day, with the Chamber of Commerce and the people in its political strategy department.

A few weeks later, eight days before the election, Indiana Governor and vice presidential candidate Mike Pence came to town. He was holding a rally in a hangar at the St. Petersburg-Clearwater airport. As the local Republican candidate for the Florida House of Representatives, it was my honor and responsibility to attend.

I arrived at the hangar wearing a blazer and a t-shirt that said *JB for Florida House*. My campaign manager secured front-row seating for me, so I was well positioned to meet the governor once he was done with his speech.

Soon Pence's plane landed. It was an antique Boeing 737, probably built around the time I walked into Pierre Trudeau's office. In fact, the plane still said *Eastern Airlines* on it. God knows how and where his campaign found it.

Pence and I have our differences. I couldn't understand why, as governor of Indiana, he wrote a law that deliberately discriminated against gay people. But on other issues, especially those related to supporting business, we agree. In fact, as I and my colleagues work to reinstate the Companionship Exemption, we plan to start by getting Mike Pence on our side.

Pence got off the plane, did the appropriate smiling and waving, and made his stump speech. When he was done, he came over to the rope line. When he reached me and saw my shirt, he said, "JB, what's going on in your race? How many points down are you?"

"About two points," I said.

"Two points? That's nothing. Why don't you pray? Tell God that you want to win by one vote. You know that you can ask God for anything. He's God. Two points for God is nothing."

For a moment, my own words from years earlier echoed in my brain. I was talking to Lisa. *You know what? God is great. He can make sure that you give birth to three strong, healthy babies if he wants to. It's no skin off his back. Let's go for it.*

"Okay," I said. "I'll pray."

And, later that day, I did. But I couldn't keep myself from adding, *Thank you for giving us healthy children. Each one matters so much more to me than winning this election.*

On election night, the television networks show you rooms crowded with chatting people, all anxiously awaiting the election results. What they don't show you are the unglamorous green rooms off to the side, where the results actually come in—and where the media's presence is forbidden. These rooms typically have a table or two, a few chairs, two or three computer monitors, and little else. That's where I and my campaign manager, Matt, were camped out.

The media also tend to draw out the process of declaring a winner. Partly it's to build suspense and keep people glued to their TVs and smartphones; partly it's because they don't want to make a mistake and get laughed at. But in real life, a lot of races can be called within half an hour after the polls close.

Early voting has changed the vote-counting process. All the early votes go into an offline queue and sit there until the polls close. The moment they close, someone in the Supervisor of Elections office hits a button, and all the early votes pop register at the same time. So Matt and I knew the complete results of all the early voting by 7:04.

Then, about ten minutes later, the results of election day voting started to come in. As we watched, the screens would suddenly update, then freeze, then slowly load, then update again as new packets of data flowed in.

By 7:20 the trends were clear: Ben Diamond had a solid lead. I was doing respectably, but I'd never be able to catch him. (In the end, Ben received 55.9% of the 75,000+ votes cast; I received 44.1%.)

Matt asked, "Well, JB, do you want to wait, or do you want me to call it?"

I said, "Let's call it. I can ring Ben, he and I can talk, and I can make my concession speech. Then we can all go and have fun."

"All right. That's the plan."

I dialed Ben Diamond's cell phone. He picked up on the first ring. "Hi, JB."

"Congratulations, Ben. You did it."

"Thank you."

"Listen," I said. "You won because you're a very, very nice guy. That got you two years in Tallahassee. But if you want to stay in office, be a centrist. No one wants you to just be a good, obedient Democrat in a Republican state. They want you to serve the people who live in Pinellas County. And nobody looks to state legislators because their life is going well. By the time they've brought their issue to you, everything is falling apart for them. You're the last stop on a very long train ride. So do what's best for the human being in front of you who asks you for help."

"Thanks, JB," Ben said. "Good advice."

I thought, *I hope you follow it. But whether you do or not, the voters will decide in 2018 whether you get to stay in.*

"JB," Ben told me, "you were a good opponent. You were pleasant, kind, funny. And I'm probably the only Democrat in the state of Florida who had to face a challenger who believes in Medicaid expansion and a woman's right to choose. You didn't give me a lot to work with in opposing you." Then he added, "The numbers were in my favor, but you clearly know what you're doing."

I thanked him, hung up, and nodded to Matt.

"Okay," he told the people around us. "JB's going to give his concession speech. Let's bring him in through the back."

As we walked through the kitchen, Matt recited a long list of people that I needed to thank. And then we were at the door to the stage.

As I entered, hundreds of people cheered and clapped. My children probably cheered the loudest.

I couldn't have been more proud. I'd been a candidate—and a serious contender—for a high-level office in the third-largest state in America.

I gave my speech, thanked everyone, and publicly wished Ben Diamond well.

The chairman of the Pinellas County Republican Party spoke, too. The essence of his talk was, *JB will be back.*

As I write these words, I'm no longer at the political candidates' table. But that's strictly temporary. I'll be back at that table soon enough, doing everything I can to win Ben Diamond's Florida House seat. These seats get voted on every two years, so it won't be too long before a new election cycle begins.

Six months ago, I was a newcomer to St. Petersburg. Now my face, name, and positions on key issues are well known throughout the district. I've built relationships with many of the movers and shakers in the region, both Republicans and Democrats, and I've got many more meetings with key people planned for the months ahead.

The Republican Party of Pinellas County continues to eagerly stand behind me. At first I worried that they'd give me flak for not strictly following the party line. They did just the opposite. They liked that I brought a new conversation—and new voters—to the party, and helped to expand its reach.

From the time I moved to St. Petersburg, no one batted an eye over the fact that my legs work less than perfectly or that I walk with two canes. Everyone notices, of course, but no one cares. That's exactly how it should be.

I still vividly recall when I walked down that long hallway four decades ago to meet with Pierre Trudeau. Now I envision a day when I'm seated in my own legislative office in the state Capitol. I hear a commotion outside, open the door, and find an agitated kid outside. "JB, I need to talk to you. What's happening to me isn't fair."

You can bet that I'll usher in that child and say, "I know just how you feel. Come in and let's figure out how I can help."

❧ OTHER KEY LESSONS ❧

- Don't assume that people have to perfectly agree with you in order to give you their support.
- Positions matter—but integrity and genuineness matter more.
- Sometimes simply showing up can be the most powerful thing to do.
- When you pray to God for favors, also give thanks.
- Don't worry too much about ideology. Instead, do what's best for the human being in front of you who needs your help.

37

If You Choose to Leave the Table, Be Clear and Honest With Yourself About Why. If You Choose to Stay, Be Equally Clear and Honest With Yourself About Your Reasons.

A t the end of Chapter 3, I wrote, *People with disabilities don't succeed when they make the shot; they succeed when they take the shot. And often they do make the shot.*

Now that we're near the end of the book, I'd like to add these observations:

Whenever you run for public office, in one sense you've already made the shot. You've said, *This is who I am. Look at me, listen to what I have to say, and then make up your mind about me. Whether you like me or dislike me, I'm here at the candidates' table, and my name is printed on your ballot.*

You've also established strong connections in the community. You've made friends, acquaintances, political partnerships, and perhaps business ones, too. You've probably made a few enemies as well—but if you ran a fair race, even your enemies will respect you. Some of them might even be your political or ideological enemies, but your personal friends. At times, these can be some of the best friends to have.

You've also made the shot if you ran for office, lost the race, and said, *Okay, I see that people don't want me, so I'm going to do something else. I'll be a writer and speaker. Or I'll make a million dollars in business. Or I'll finally do whatever it is I've most wanted to do.* That's a win, too, because you understand your situation, know what the next thing to do is, and have the chance to succeed in some other way. In the end, you might end up at a far better table than the one you tried to get elected to.

Or maybe, if you're like me, you made the shot when you decided to go the distance. You're not thinking in terms of winning one election. You've got a long-term plan for getting to the table. This might require two or three runs for the same office, until you've earned the trust and respect of enough people to win the majority of their votes. That's my game plan.

This is why, on election night, I felt like a winner. I had run a fair and respectful campaign. Most of the people in my district now knew who I was. Many also knew what I stood for—and that it was not the standard script out of any party's playbook. Even though I had only lived in the area for six months, while my opponent had grown up there, and had recently returned to run for public office, I received 44% of the vote. Lots of people told me, "The wrong candidate won." Lots of others said to me, "JB, you're the only Republican I voted for." I had successfully taken the biggest and most important step toward getting elected to the Florida House of Representatives. The future had become one step closer and easier.

That's the beauty of running for office. If you don't make it to the table this time around, you can take another shot in the following election.

Here is the text my 16-year-old daughter Rena sent me on election night, shortly after we knew the results of the vote:

Hi daddy!! You were a winner from the beginning! You never let anyone step over you or walk over you in any way! All though we lost we're coming back for 2018 to kick his butt now you got a business to go run!! And show them how it's done:) i know u say i'm ur favorite but today i actually got to experience the favoritism and meant it. everyone knew who i was ONLY BECAUSE OF THE FAMOUS DADDY!! I got to appreciate you in every way possible not only of how u inspire everyone around you but as my dad to learn and grow from you in every way possible!!... I love you So So So So much and ur the real winner!! ♥ ♥ ♥#2018

I received similar messages from all of my children. In fact, they continue to routinely let me and their mother know that, in their minds, we are rock stars.

Earlier in this book I wrote about advocates and protectors. Having any one of these on your side is a blessing. Having all of them surrounding you, as I do, is a miracle.

And if you're really, really lucky, you might also have a personal cheerleader.

Your cheerleader is not someone who cheers really loud or waves pom poms in your face. It's the person who whispers in your ear, *I love you, JB. Go get 'em. You've got this.* Even when they know success still has many challenges ahead.

My kids turned out to be the best cheerleaders I've ever had. And I'm blessed to have four of them.

As you've seen, I've devoted my life to being included, to getting to one table after another. I'm happy to say that, most of the time, I've succeeded. Most people with disabilities aren't so fortunate.

Exclusion always hurts real, living, flesh-and-blood people. When you choose not to give a job to the most qualified applicant because they're disabled, it doesn't just exclude them and diminish their ability to earn a living. It also diminishes their trust in other human beings and their confidence in themselves. It also deprives the world of their talents.

If you're walking with your six-year-old daughter through the mall, and she points at someone like me and asks loudly, "Why is that person walking funny?," don't shush her, or yank on her arm and pull her in the other direction. If you do that, you're excluding the disabled person *and* your daughter.

Instead, you can say, "They've got a condition they were born with that makes them walk that way. Most people walk like you and me, but some people are born different, so they walk different."

Or, if the disabled person doesn't seem in a hurry, you can say to your daughter, "Let's find out." You can lead your daughter to the person and say, "Excuse me. My daughter is curious about why you walk differently than she does. Would you be willing to explain it to her?" If the person has the time, they'll usually be happy to answer.

I do this with kids all the time. When I hear a child ask, "Why is that man walking with two canes?," I normally stop, smile at the child, and say, "Because it's much easier for me with two canes."

This makes perfect sense to kids, perhaps because they're young enough to remember when they first learned to walk. They either say, "Oh," or, sometimes, "Oh. Okay. Thanks, mister."

I can also tell you this: when a child asks that kind of question in public, the disabled person hears it. The question doesn't bother us at all. But when an adult shushes the child or pulls them away, that *does* bother us.

In one sense, my disability has been a gift. When you're not accepted at certain tables, you naturally learn to think differently. You get very creative about devising ways to get to the table you have your heart set on. And once you're there, you make a point of helping others to join you—or to get to other tables that interest them. Most of all, you never take your place at any table for granted.

It turns out that these principles apply to everyone who wants to lead a meaningful life. Paradoxically, those of us with disabilities usually learn them at a young age. It's our fellow able-bodied human beings who seem to have the most difficulty learning them and living by them.

So, for you and for everyone else reading this book, here are those principles again:

Be creative.
Help others.
Don't take your blessings for granted.

❈ OTHER KEY LESSONS ❈

- When you say, *I tried X and failed, so I'm not doing it anymore; I'm going to do Y instead*, you may have taken a big step toward your future success.
- When you say, *I tried X and failed, so I'm going to try again— but I'll use what I've learned to do X better next time*, you may have *also* taken a big step toward your future success.
- If you have a personal cheerleader in your life, be deeply grateful for them.
- Remember that unfair or arbitrary exclusion doesn't just harm the excluded person. It also harms the person doing the excluding—and, often, innocent bystanders as well.

38

When Someone Else Has to Leave the Table, Help Them Leave Graciously and With Dignity

A s I observed earlier, each of us belongs in this world, simply because we were born into it. But for each of us, there will also come a time when we have to leave it.

My father David was known for his kindness, his advocacy, and his deep caring and concern for others. So it strikes me as appropriate that when he died, the people around him—including complete strangers—expressed that same concern.

On the morning of Saturday, December 16, 2000, my dad woke up feeling sick. He called his doctor's office and was told, "Come over and we'll fit you in." So he walked more than a mile to his doctor's office, through the falling snow.

Why didn't my father drive? No one knows. Normally he would have driven. Many Orthodox Jews don't drive on *Shabbat*, but my father routinely did. Maybe he felt too sick. Maybe he felt the fresh air would help.

The doctor checked my father's vital signs and told him, "You've got a bad cold. Here, get this prescription filled. Start taking it, get plenty of rest, drink lots of fluids, and you'll be fine."

My father did as he was advised. After lunch, while my mother went out briefly to visit a friend, he lay down for a nap.

The Jewish Sabbath ends at sundown on Saturday. Just before the end of every *Shabbat*, my parents would drive to my sister Karina's home a few miles away, where they would share a meal and perform a brief ritual called *Havdalah*, which marks the end of *Shabbat* and the beginning of the new week. In Montreal in December, the sun sets very early. Shabbat ends around 5 p.m., so my parents needed to leave by 4.

When my mother returned, she took off her shoes and coat and called out, "David! We need to leave in a few minutes!" She waited for his reply, but none came.

Figuring that her husband was still sleeping, my mom went into their bedroom. She saw my dad lying face down on the floor, as if he were doing pushups, wearing nothing but his pajama bottoms.

"David," she said, "Get up. We have to go to Karina's. We're going to be late if we don't leave soon."

When he didn't reply, she knew that something was very wrong.

She ran to the kitchen, filled a pitcher with water, and threw the water on her husband's body. He didn't move.

My mom knew that some of our relatives would be gathering at the nearby synagogue for their own *Havdalah* service. She didn't stop to put on her shoes. She ran barefoot six blocks to the synagogue. There she found two of my cousins. She told them, "I think something's wrong with Uncle David."

They ran back to my parents' home. My father still hadn't moved. My cousins checked his vital signs. He wasn't breathing and he had no pulse. His body was already beginning to cool.

My cousin Leon recited the *Shema*, the most basic Hebrew prayer, over my father's body. My cousin Moses called an ambulance. My mother called a friend and asked her to call Karina and explain that our father had been taken to the hospital.

By the time the ambulance got my father to the nearest emergency room, it was clear to everyone—my mother, my cousins, and the EMTs—that there was no hope for his resuscitation. He was pronounced dead on arrival at Sacre-Coeur Hospital.

My mother and cousins called their rabbi, and waited for him to arrive and recite a final blessing.

While they waited, the hospital did something very compassionate and caring. They said to my mother, "Mrs. Bensmihen, the emergency room is busy and noisy and crowded. Let's put your husband in a regular patient room, where you and your family can have some privacy and quiet."

My mother agreed. Orderlies put my father on a gurney, transported him up to a private room, and put his body into a bed. Then they left to let my family talk, grieve, pray, and wait for the rabbi.

What the staff of Sacre-Coeur Hospital did was what we Jews call a *chesed*, a blessing. It was also a *mitzvah*, a kind and compassionate deed.

Of course, my family didn't use those words with the staff at a Catholic hospital (*Sacre-Coeur* means "sacred cross"). My mother and cousins simply said, "Thank you."

This wasn't just an act of thoughtfulness and kindness. It was also an act of sacrifice, because my family was taking up a room that the hospital could otherwise have put a patient in, and billed the province for.

The hospital helped my father leave this world with grace and dignity. It also helped my family have their own dignity as they said goodbye.

We didn't do an autopsy, so we don't know precisely how my father died. But bad hearts run in the Bensmihen bloodline, so we're pretty sure he died of heart failure.

In a sense this is a huge irony, because my father David had one of the biggest and most compassionate hearts of any human being on this planet. To this day I'm grateful that he was my father.

Rest in peace, Dad. Even today, your words of love and support still echo in my heart and head:

Joseph, you're the best.

⬥ OTHER KEY LESSONS ⬥

- Thoughtfulness and kindness are blessings. When they are combined with sacrifice, they become holy.
- Don't wait until later to do good deeds—or to work toward taking your place at the table. You don't know when your life will end. Your time on Earth is precious. Use it wisely and well.

Afterword

Your Place at the Table Awaits

I haven't walked in your particular shoes. I don't even know if you can walk. I also don't know what specific challenges you face.

I do know, though, that every one of us face challenges. All of us have limitations. And in some ways, all of us are outsiders. None of us belongs at every table.

But all of us do belong in this world. This includes you. You also belong at certain tables, even if some people tell you that you don't.

I can't know what those specific tables are. But you can. So, please, get as clear as you can about what they are. Then learn how a place at each of them is acquired.

Then do some strategizing. Pick the tables that look like good investments of your time and energy—and where your odds of success look decent. The guidance, stories, and strategies in this book can help.

Sometimes, though, it's worth shooting for a table that seems far out of reach, or where the odds of getting to it seem small. This makes sense when you don't need to invest much effort or time, or when you have nothing to lose and much to gain by trying. (Think of my trip to meet Prime Minister Trudeau when I was six.)

And, when possible, have a Plan B (and possibly a Plan C) in mind, in case things don't work out.

I've done well in business, so here's a success secret for my fellow business owners:

Disabled people often make the best employees. We want so much to contribute that when we're given a chance, we work tremendously hard. We're extremely loyal. We don't take for granted things such as training, mentoring, and performance reviews. And we're eager to do well and succeed. As a result, hiring the disabled may give you an edge on your competition.

Sure, there are some duds among us, but the percentage is no higher than it is among people in general. In fact, it's probably lower, because the duds tend to stay home.

For everyone, here's a final tip:

Every day is a new day. No matter who you are, or what you've gone through, or what mistakes you've made, or where you've been, you always have the opportunity to start anew.

And if you happen to see a Moroccan-looking guy with two canes in an airport, or at a conference, or in the halls of Congress, don't just smile at him and walk past. Shout out to him, "Hey, JB! Who's the best?"

If it's me, I'll turn, smile, and shout back, "You are!"

About the Author

Joseph Bensmihen is widely known as JB—and, sometimes, as the guy with two canes who advises members of Congress.

JB was born with cerebral palsy. At age six, unhappy with being denied a place in a regular elementary school, he walked into Prime Minister Pierre Trudeau's office, asked for an immediate meeting with him, and got it.

He was in the news five years later, when he became the first disabled Canadian student to be mainstreamed in a public school. The press coverage turned international a few years afterward, when he gave the valedictorian speech at his high school graduation. At age 22, JB was back in the news again, when the Americans with Disabilities Act went into effect, and he published a widely discussed opinion piece for the *Montreal Gazette*, urging Canada to follow America's lead.

Over the past decade, JB has advised multiple members of Congress—Congressman Eric Cantor (R), Congressman Ted Deutch (D), Congressman Dennis Ross (R), Congressman Jim Langevin (D), Congressman Tom Rooney (R), and Congressman Patrick Murphy (D)—and former senator Mary Landrieu (D). Topics have included health care, consumer rights, the sustainability of small businesses, and American-Israeli relations. He has also met with three presidents— Clinton, Bush, and Obama—Vice President Mike Pence, and multiple senators. In 2013, he testified before the U.S. House Committee on Education and the Workforce on affordable care for seniors and people with disabilities.

He is the former President of the Private Care Association, a national association that supports consumer choice in private health care and the rights of caregivers who serve those consumers. He also directs the David Bensmihen Charitable Foundation, which provides scholarships for deserving students. For five years he has been a member of the Board of Overseers for the men's undergraduate college at Yeshiva University. Until 2014, when he sold the business, he was the CEO of United Elder Care Services, a company providing home health care in south Florida.

On January 24, 2016, he walked (with two canes) in the Miami Marathon. He also served as the master of ceremonies for the marathon's kickoff event the evening before.

In 2016, he ran as a centrist Republican for a seat in the Florida House of Representatives in District 68, located in St. Petersburg and some of its suburbs. JB received 44% of all votes—an unusually high number for a newcomer to the area. He is already planning a second run for a Florida House seat in 2018 or 2020.

JB has given hundreds of inspirational talks at a wide range of venues, from Chautauqua Institute to Yeshiva University. He is a regular presenter around the United States for Friendship Circle, a Jewish organization that supports inclusion for people with disabilities (friendshipcircle.org).

He has received Yeshiva University's Points of Light award and multiple Distinguished Community Service Awards from Florida Atlantic University's School of Social Work.

Currently, JB serves as Vice President of Evergreen Private Care and lives in St. Petersburg, Florida.

Morgan James
Speakers Group

◢ www.TheMorganJamesSpeakersGroup.com

We connect Morgan James published
authors with live and online events
and audiences who will benefit
from their expertise.

Morgan James makes all of our titles available
through the Library for All Charity Organization.

www.LibraryForAll.org

Printed in the USA
CPSIA information can be obtained
at www.ICGtesting.com
JSHW022327140824
68134JS00019B/1342